BOWLING

BROWN

PHYSICAL EDUCATION ACTIVITIES SERIES

Consulting Editor:

AILEENE LOCKHART
University of Southern California
Los Angeles, California

Evaluation Materials Editor:

JANE A. MOTT
Smith College
Northampton, Massachusetts

ARCHERY, Wayne C. McKinney
BADMINTON, Margaret Varner
BIOPHYSICAL VALUES OF MUSCULAR ACTIVITY, E. C. Davis,
    Gene A. Logan, and Wayne C. McKinney
BOWLING, Joan Martin
CIRCUIT TRAINING, Robert P. Sorani
CONDITIONING AND BASIC MOVEMENT CONCEPTS, Jane A. Mott
CONTEMPORARY SQUARE DANCE, Patricia A. Phillips
FENCING, Muriel Bower and Torao Mori
FIELD HOCKEY, Anne Delano
FIGURE SKATING, Marion Proctor
FOLK DANCE, Lois Ellfeldt
GOLF, Virginia L. Nance and E. C. Davis
HANDBALL, Michael Yessis
JUDO, Daeshik Kim
LACROSSE FOR GIRLS AND WOMEN, Anne Delano
BASKETBALL FOR MEN, Glenn Wilkes
GYMNASTICS FOR MEN, A. Bruce Frederick
MODERN DANCE, Esther E. Pease
PHYSICAL AND PHYSIOLOGICAL CONDITIONING FOR MEN, Benjamin Ricci
SKIING, Clayne Jensen and Karl Tucker
SKIN AND SCUBA DIVING, Albert A. Tillman
SOCCER, Richard L. Nelson
SOCIAL DANCE, William F. Pillich
SOFTBALL, Martin E. Kneer and Charles L. McCord
SQUASH RACQUETS, Margaret Varner and Norman Bramall
SWIMMING, Betty J. Vickers and William J. Vincent
TABLE TENNIS, Margaret Varner and J. R. Harrison
TAP DANCE, Barbara Nash
TENNIS, Joan Johnson and Paul Xanthos
TRACK AND FIELD, Kenneth E. Foreman and Virginia L. Husted
TRAMPOLINING, Jeff T. Hennessy
VOLLEYBALL, Glen H. Egstrom and Frances Schaafsma
WEIGHT TRAINING, Philip J. Rasch
BASKETBALL FOR WOMEN, Frances Schaafsma
GYMNASTICS FOR WOMEN, A. Bruce Frederick
WRESTLING, Arnold Umbach and Warren R. Johnson

PHYSICAL EDUCATION

ACTIVITIES SERIES

BOWLING

JOAN L. MARTIN

Associate Supervisor of Physical Education
University of California, Los Angeles

WM. C. BROWN COMPANY PUBLISHERS
DUBUQUE, IOWA

Preface

Bowling is rapidly becoming the leading participating sport for all ages of Americans, teen-agers, college students, the working class, family groups and senior citizens. This book is designed to assist these eager enthusiasts, particularly the students, in learning the basic skills and knowledges which lead to optimum bowling performance.

There is no substitute for good instruction in the learning process, but good instruction also profits from reinforcement by the written word and visual cues. Most of today's students seek and appreciate opportunities to find out more and more about what they are attempting to learn or do. They require an explanation of the "why" and the "when" as well as the "how to."

The material presented delves into all aspects of the game including its early history and development, values, popularity, official rules, scoring, etiquette, bowler's language, equipment and facilities.

Although the emphasis is primarily on the novice, the experienced bowler will discover many helpful hints to assist him in correcting faults in his approach or delivery, adjusting to differences in lane conditions, some thoughts on strategies and points of concentration for competitive bowling.

Self-evaluation questions are distributed throughout this text. These afford the reader typical examples of the kinds of understanding and levels of skill that he should be acquiring as he progresses toward proficiency in bowling. The player should not only answer the printed questions but should pose additional ones as a self-check on learning. In some instances the student may find that he cannot respond fully and accurately to a question until he has read more extensively or has gained more playing experience. From time to time he should return to such troublesome questions until he is sure of the answers or has developed the skills called for, as the case may be.

Many generous friends, colleagues, and students assisted me in the preparation of the manuscript, photographs and illustrations. My deepest gratitude to Dr. Ruth Abernathy for editing the manuscript, to Peggy Iden for her assistance in photography and typing, to Ann Stutts for the illustrations, and to Don Sawyer, director of the Student Union Bowling Lanes for his cooperation and valuable suggestions.

My sincere thanks and appreciation to the kind and patient students who performed so well for the photographs, Bill Lewis, Lynne Schwab and Anita Bergford, and to Mike DeAngelo for his cooperation in the use of the lanes and equipment.

I am also indebted to the American Bowling Congress, the Women's International Bowling Congress, AMF and Brunswick for supplying me with valuable information and materials.

JOAN MARTIN

Contents

CHAPTER   PAGE

1. What Bowling Is Like 1

2. Skills Essential for Everyone 6

3. Better Players Master These Techniques 22

4. Progress Can Be Speeded Up 40

5. The Language and Lore of Bowling 46

6. Scoring and Rules of the Game 54

7. Unwritten Laws 60

8. Facts for Enthusiasts 63

9. Playing the Game 66

Index 70

1

What Bowling is Like

PURPOSE OF THE GAME

Bowling appears to be a very simple maneuver of rolling a large, heavy ball down a wooden lane at a grouping of ten wooden pins set up in triangular formation at the end of the lane. The object of the game is to knock down as many pins as possible in ten frames. Each frame involves one or two attempts (the tenth frame may involve three attempts). The score is the total number of pins knocked down in the ten frames (plus bonuses). A perfect game of 300 is scored by knocking down all pins with the first ball rolled in each frame ("strike") with two extra balls allowed for a strike in the tenth frame. A low score in the 70's or 80's may result if an inexperienced bowler needs two balls in each frame, then very seldom knocks down all the pins in the two attempts and receives no bonuses for strikes or spares.

A team for league competition consists of four or five bowlers. Systems of handicapping allow for equalized competition.

VALUES

Bowling has gained respectability and prestige within the past twenty years, so much so that it has become one of the most popular sports for participants of all ages, regardless of sex, size, shape, physical condition and, in fact, for the physically handicapped as well. Due largely to the promotional and supervisorial efforts of the American Bowling Congress, bowling has graduated from a sport of "bums" to a sport of kings, queens and also just plain folks.

Bowling is not a strenuous game; physical strength is not a limiting factor, and anyone can bowl inexpensively. Most bowling centers today furnish balls free, rent shoes at a nominal fee, and may also furnish free instruction in the fundamentals. The skills used in bowling are not too complicated for average performance and enjoyment. Going bowling requires less time in preparation, transportation to and from, and in actual participation than do golf, skiing, swimming, riding, etc. These considera-

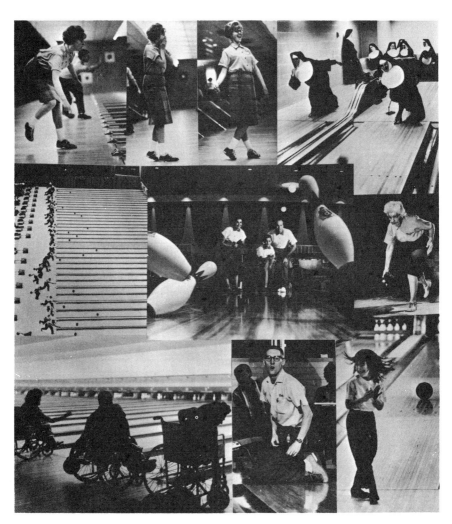

Figure 1—Everybody Bowls (Courtesy of Brunswick Corporation)

tions make bowling an excellent activity for a busy family get-to-gether where time is a limiting factor in the tempo of modern city living.

The informal nature of the game allows for socializing and chit-chat between turns; in addition, league bowling affords an opportunity to make many new friends and acquaintances as teams meet different opponents each week.

The time permitted between turns for relaxation and socializing is balanced by a need for real concentration and mental alertness to judge certain spare pickups and strategies of the game when your turn comes along. Bowling offers a constant challenge and watching one's own ball control and average improve can be a great personal satisfaction whether bowling informally with family or in a highly competitive league.

Although bowling is not a strenuous activity, it nevertheless demands enough physical exertion to be classified as an enjoyable moderate exercise for maintaining muscle fitness. It is a safe sport and the probability of injury is slight.

Figure 2—Modern Bowling Center (Courtesy of Brunswick Corporation)

POPULARITY

That bowling is the most popular indoor sport today is evidenced by the fact that over a billion dollars is spent on bowling every year by 35,000,000 bowlers in 158,000 certified lanes throughout the country. The increase in the number of women bowlers is fantastic. From 5,000 registered in 1927, the Women's International Bowling Congress reports it now has 2,650,000 women bowlers.

As a service to increase the youth fitness program and to add more carry-over skills to the physical education classes, one of the leading bowling manufacturers has developed a "Learn to Bowl" kit for instructor's use in the gymnasium. Three and a half million students have thus far learned to bowl, and it is expected that eventually 15 million will be reached by this service. College student union buildings are adding bowling facilities at a rapid rate to provide recreation and league competition for students, faculty and employees.

Bowling appeals more to people in their twenties than any other age bracket. Twenty-six per cent of all those who bowl are between 20 and 29 years of age; second with 22 per cent are the teen-agers (15 to 19 years). The American Junior Bowling Congress has done much in the way of furnishing free instruction and competitive events for young bowlers.

Television has been a boon to bowling and has helped to interest thousands of TV sports watchers and encourage them to learn the game. The televised tournaments and money matches have encouraged many skilled bowlers to turn "pro." TV has helped to spread enthusiasm for the sport and has greatly supplemented the promotional efforts of the American Bowling Congress. The pro bowlers have not yet reached the money ranks of the pro golfers, but they are gaining. The leading pros who bowl on the tournament trail and on television may earn upwards of $50,000 a year. In 1965 for the first open event outside the North American continent the pros participated in a tournament in Caracas, Venezuela.

EQUIPMENT

A unique feature about bowling is that you can learn and develop a taste for the game without purchasing any equipment. As previously mentioned, most bowling centers rent shoes for a nominal fee and furnish a variety of balls from which you can select one suitable for learning purposes. If you wish to take up bowling in earnest, you should purchase a ball custom-fitted to your hand and grip. Details for the purchase of personal equipment will be found in Chapter 8.

Most commercial lanes charge thirty-five to fifty-five cents a line, depending on the locale, the spaciousness of the establishment and services offered by the proprietor. Original construction outlay, about a thousand dollars per lane, and the high maintenance costs of keeping the lanes and pin machines in top shape necessitate higher bowling fees in some areas.

A regulation lane or alley consists of the approach, which is a minimum of 15 feet in length and extends to the foul line; the foul line dividing the approach and the alley bed; and the alley bed itself which extends from the foul line 63 feet to the pit end where the pins are set down and removed by the automatic machines. The gutters at either side of the alley bed which catch misdirected balls, the ball return and the rack are also parts of a complete lane.

Regulation lanes are contructed of maple and pine boards set on edge in order to make a solid, durable surface which will withstand much wear. The first 12 to 15 feet of the lane are maple; the pine boards which are a softer more porous wood are used from the "range finder" area to the pins. The pine boards make possible more ball action or spin. Range finders are the dark brown arrows built into the bed to serve as points of aim for "spot" bowlers.

Lane conditions vary considerably according to the manner in which they are finished and maintained. Some lanes which have just been oiled are called "holding lanes" meaning they are fast and cut down on the amount of hook on the ball; others may be slow or "running" and the hook will break too much and too soon. The experienced bowler after rolling a practice ball or two can determine or "read" the alley and can make adjustments in his point of aim or in the technique of his delivery which will accommodate the ball to the type or condition of the lane.

Bowling pins usually are made of maple or laminated wood, weigh from three to three and one-half pounds each and are 15 inches high. The specifications on size and weight of pins is rigidly controlled by the A.B.C. They must be unusually durable to withstand a 2,000 pound blow each time a bowling ball, traveling on the average of 15 miles per hour, makes a direct hit on a pin. A pin will last an average of 5,000 games.

Regulation balls have a circumference of 27 inches, may weigh from 10 to 16 pounds and have two or three finger holes drilled to fit an individual's grip and type of delivery. See Chapter 8 for details of a bowler's personal equipment including ball, shoes, bag and clothing.

Skills Essential for Everyone

Learning to bowl is largely a matter of developing the concept of rolling the ball smoothly at the proper angle to topple the pins instead of slamming the ball at them. To accomplish the "smooth roll" successfully, the learner must abandon his natural inclination to slam the ball down the alley with as much force as he can muster. This offers a problem to men who like speed. A ball thrown with uncontrolled speed is rarely synonymous with a strike ball. The weight of the ball and the distance to the pins are apt to make the beginner think that the faster he rolls the ball the sooner it will get to the pins without deviation, and that the more force it carries the more pins will go down. While a certain amount of ball speed is necessary to knock the pins over, excessive speed causes the pins to fly up and off the alley instead of allowing the chain reaction of one pin hitting against another pin until all topple over. Of course, it is essential that the ball hit the pins at the correct spot for the chain reaction to produce a strike!

Before you ever lift a bowling ball to try the game, set your mind toward the objective of learning to "roll" a smooth, well-controlled ball.

PREPARATION

Now that the challenge of rolling a smooth, well-controlled ball is clear in your mind there are a few preliminary steps to be taken before you step up to roll the ball.

First, dress appropriately to allow for freedom of movement. Bowling does not require a special costume and for men, everyday clothing is

Pins "Topple"—Correct   *Pins "Fly"—Incorrect*

Figure 3

satisfactory. Women should wear skirts which will allow for the knee bend and stretch in the sliding motion at delivery, neither too narrow nor too full. Blouses should be loose through the shoulders to permit a free arm swing. Bowling shoes are required in most bowling establishments and can be rented as previously mentioned. Check out shoes, reserve a lane, and secure a score sheet at the check out desk before going to a lane. Fees are paid upon the completion of your bowling when you return the score sheet and shoes to the desk.

Take time in selecting a ball from the rack so that you find one that is suitable in weight, span, and size of finger and thumb holes. House balls are usually arranged on the rack according to number and weight, and in addition may have the weight stamped on the ball. If you have never bowled before, probably all balls will seem heavy. In general, men should select a ball in the 14 to 16 pound range and women in the 10 to 12 pound range. The regulation maximum weight of a bowling ball is 16 and the minimum is 10 pounds. Lighter balls are made for juniors.

More important than the weight of the ball is the way it is fit to the hand. While "fit" is an individual matter, the method of determining the fit varies, depending on the type of grip chosen. There are three basic types of bowling grips—conventional, semi-finger tip, and finger tip. See Figure 4. In the conventional or standard grip which should be used in learning to bowl, the second and third fingers are inserted to the second joint. In the semi-finger tip grip the fingers are inserted to midway between the first and second joint, and in the full finger tip the fingers are inserted to the first joint only.

7

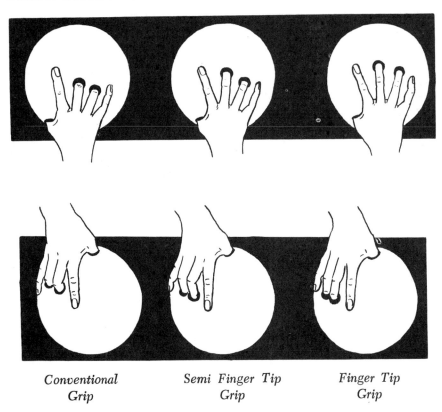

| Conventional Grip | Semi Finger Tip Grip | Finger Tip Grip |

Figure 4—Three Types of Balls

The thumb hole should allow the thumb to slide in and out freely. Test this by inserting the thumb all the way in the hole and turning it rapidly clockwise and counterclockwise. If this can be done with very little friction, then the thumb fit is proper. To determine the correct span or distance between the thumb hole and finger holes, insert the thumb as far as possible in the thumb hole and extend the hand and fingers over the contour of the ball so the fingers stretch over the holes as shown in Figure 5. The second joint of the middle finger should extend approximately ¼″ beyond the inside edge of the finger hole. Do not forcibly stretch the hand in checking the span. Left-handed bowlers should look for balls marked "L.H." in order to have the correct location of the middle finger hole. It is set in about ¼″ closer to the thumb hole than is the ring finger hole.

When you have found a ball that seems to fit comfortably test it by gripping it and swinging it back and forth in a pendulum swing motion, then try one or two more balls and choose the one which feels best. The real test is in rolling it, however, and you may wish to try out different balls the first few times you bowl. Be particular, select the best available fit for you until you can purchase your own ball and have it drilled to fit your hand and grip.

A word of caution in picking the ball off the ball return—to eliminate the possibility of finger injury and strain, get the habit of picking up your ball from the return with both hands. Extend the hands on opposite sides of the ball away from any oncoming balls and lift the ball from the return as though there were no holes in it. Always face the alley as you pick up the ball. See Figure 6.

Picking the ball up with the fingers in the holes is not only fatiguing and a strain on the fingers and arm but there is more possibility of dropping it on the approach, or worse yet, on your foot.

Figure 5—Checking the Span

Figure 6—Correct Way to Lift Ball from Rack

BASIC SKILLS

Much of your success in bowling will depend on how well the preliminary actions necessary to the smooth, well-controlled delivery of the ball are mastered. As in any sport, learning and practicing the fundamental movement patterns are necessary in order to project a ball toward a given target as efficiently and accurately as possible. For the average person there is no short cut to eventual optimum performance in an activity except through understanding of and dedicated practice in the fundamentals leading up to the actual projection of the ball or object. The preparatory actions, coordination of arm and leg patterns, the application of force, timing and balance are as important in delivering a bowling ball as in putting the shot or serving a tennis ball. You can build on the required fundamental movements a certain style or minor unique action pattern better suited to your individual make-up, but the basic skills remain much the same for everyone.

Keep in mind that all directions are given in terms of right-handed bowlers. Left handers should adjust the phrasing to suit them.

The Starting Position—The starting position can reflect individual preference as long as it is comfortable and relaxed. There are no hard and fast rules on how to address the pins except that you should face the target squarely, with your shoulders at a right angle on an imaginary line from shoulders to target. Fix your eyes on the target or spot for which you are aiming. A more detailed explanation of spot bowling will appear in the following chapter. The position of your feet and the height at which the ball is held vary. See Figure 7. You may need to experiment with different stances and ball positions before you decide on one best suited to your timing and strength.

Determine where to stand in relation to distance from the foul line and distance from the right side of the approach. The proper distance

Figure 7—Three Stances

for you to start from the foul line can be paced off by standing with your back to the alley bed at the foul line and walking four and one half normal walking steps toward the beginning of the approach. The half step allows for the slide as you roll the ball. Note the spot at which you arrive. The position toward center from the right side of the alley varies with the type of ball rolled. Until you have practiced enough to know what kind of ball (straight, hook, curve, or back-up) you will be rolling, it is safe to assume a position on the right side of the approach. The general inclination is to stand in the center and roll the ball down the middle of the alley bed at the center of the pins, but the strategic angle is from right to left for right-hand bowlers. Such an angle with slight individual variations allows for maximum toppling of pins. The angle and points of aim will be discussed in the following chapter.

Once you have experimented with several starting positions and have developed enough control and consistency to know how your ball is going to roll and what path it will take to the pins, then on each ball rolled you must check the starting position of your feet in order to improve your consistency and control. Check your heels or toes in relation to certain boards or the brown dots on the approach. It is essential that you stand on the same boards each time you roll the first ball of a frame. Depending upon the results of the first ball (that is, the position of the remaining pins) you may need to change your starting position for the second ball. These changes for the second ball will be taken up under spare bowling techniques.

The ball should be held close to the body at chest or waist height and slightly to the right of the center of the body. Support the weight of the ball with both hands and insert the fingers and then the thumb in the holes in that order, remembering to grip a little more firmly with the fingers than with the thumb. Feet should be a few inches apart and on a line parallel with the target or spot, or the left foot may be a few inches ahead for a normal four-step approach. To make sure you get started on the correct foot, shift most of your weight to the left foot prior to taking the first step with your right. Bending slightly forward from the hips can be helpful in starting your forward approach with the push away of the ball. An erect stance is also acceptable. The important point is to feel comfortable, to relax and to concentrate on the target.

To assist in relaxation as you assume the starting position, try taking a deep breath and exhaling slowly, then look to your right and left to be sure there will be no distractions from other bowlers to upset your concentration as you make the approach to deliver the ball.

11

The Approach—Four Step—The approach is the method of building up momentum for delivery of the ball by taking four walking steps forward in coordination with a pendulum-like swing of the right arm. See Figure 8.

Figure 8—Four Step Approach—Arm Swing and Step Pattern

Before concentrating on the mechanics of the approach, keep in mind that (1) speed is not the essential factor, (2) you are going to progress toward the foul line at a moderate pace rather than "charge" the foul line, and (3) you will prepare to "roll" the ball instead of "throwing" it.

The four-step approach, while not the only one, is recommended and used by at least ninety per cent of the star bowlers. If you have tried to bowl without instruction, you may have fallen into a three-step or even a five-step pattern. Unless you have bowled for a number of years using one of these, or a qualified instructor has allowed you to continue an odd step pattern because of your unusual ability or success with it, you should learn the four-step approach. It is more rhythmic than the other approaches. If you are using the three-step approach at present and are not too successful with it, or if you have tried the four-step and get overly confused, try the five-step which allows you more time to let the ball swing back. Both the three- and the five-step approach start with the first step on the left foot and it is sometimes easier though ultimately less efficient for three steppers to change to a five than to a four-step. The three-step is the least desirable of the approaches.

Next you must decide whether you are going to learn to roll a straight ball, a hook ball or a back up. Just as the four-step approach is recommended by most expert bowlers so is the hook delivery. The various types of deliveries are shown in Figure 9.

Men bowlers and the majority of women bowlers should learn the hook delivery from the very beginning. Some instructors recommend that women in particular learn to roll a straight ball first and then change over to a hook after they have mastered the fundamentals and have adequate control. Unless a student has very small or weak hands and wrists, or the hook delivery seems terribly awkward, he might as well begin with the technique and delivery to be used eventually.

Now back to the approach. After you have assumed the proper and relaxed starting position, hold the ball in both hands at a comfortable height in front of you and slightly to the right of the midline of the body. The left hand is under the ball supporting most of its weight. The right hand grips the ball in the hook delivery position. The easiest way to describe the hand position for delivering a hook is to drop your arms to your sides. Now bend the right elbow so the lower arm swings up toward the right shoulder without changing the hand position. This will result in the "handshake" or hook position of the thumb and fingers. This is the most natural of the various hand positions or grips. If you concen-

13

Can you identify the type of ball delivery shown in the diagram?

Evaluation Questions

TYPE OF DELIVERY

trate on keeping the wrist firm, holding this same hand position through-out the entire arm swing pattern and until after the ball is released, you will have no difficulty in rolling a hook.

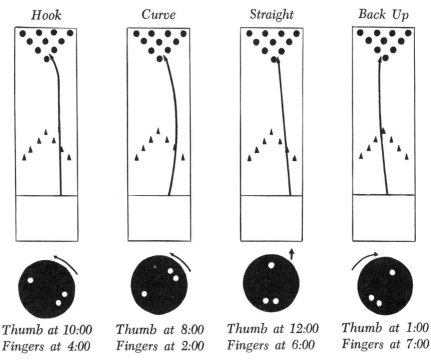

Hook	*Curve*	*Straight*	*Back Up*
Thumb at 10:00	*Thumb at 8:00*	*Thumb at 12:00*	*Thumb at 1:00*
Fingers at 4:00	*Fingers at 2:00*	*Fingers at 6:00*	*Fingers at 7:00*

Figure 9—Four Types of Deliveries

Diagram A:

TYPE OF DELIVERY

To make sure you have the correct hand position prior to starting your approach, lift the ball from the rack as described earlier and turn the thumb and finger holes to their respective positions as shown in the first diagram of Figure 9. The thumb hole should be at approximately "ten o'clock" and the finger holes at the "four o'clock" position. Insert the fingers first, then the thumb. Holding the ball comfortably in front and slightly to the right side of you as described earlier under "Starting Position," check to see the wrist, arm and hand form a fairly straight line and that the elbows are close to the body.

From the stationary starting position, take a trial swing by pushing the ball forward, down, back and forward again in a pendulum-like swing motion from the shoulder. Try this several times, feeling the ball swinging from the end of your arm. Do not attempt to lift or force the ball on the back swing. The arm should be straight and the hook grip maintained throughout the swing. There should be no rotation of the trunk, arm, or wrist during any part of this motion.

Once you are satisfied that the ball can swing smoothly and easily and have made sure the "V" formed by the thumb and first finger has remained on top of the ball during the forward swing, then the more complicated coordination can be attempted. This involves fitting the step pattern with the arm swing pattern. If the arm swing is natural, smooth, and continuous, then your attention can be devoted to the four steps taken in time with the complete arm swing.

If the first step of the approach is taken simultaneously with the push away forward motion of the ball, the next three steps should coincide with the arm swing action in rhythmic sequence. This step is the most

15

Can you maintain a firm wrist position as you swing the ball back and forth for practice?

Evaluation Questions

important one of the entire approach. As you push the ball out on a slightly downward angle at your right side, both hands supporting the ball, feel that the swing of the ball outward is causing your body to be pulled forward into taking the first short step on the right foot. If you first

Figure 10—First Step—Push Away

Figure 11—Second Step

think of starting the ball and then move the right foot to make the short initial step almost instantaneously, you will have the correct timing. If you step and then move the ball forward, or even think about the step prior to moving the ball, you will probably be "out of time" and arrive at the foul line before you're ready to release the ball. Persons who hold the ball high in front of the chin or chest for the starting position should be particularly aware of the need to move the ball out just a fraction ahead of the first step. This is necessitated by the longer distance the ball must travel before it reaches the perpendicular in the arc, by which time the second step of the approach has been completed.

Inexperienced bowlers tend to move the body toward the foul line before moving the ball and carry the ball along on the first step. Let the forward swing of the weighted ball "pull" you into the initial step. If timing is off at this point, you can be sure timing will be off at the foul line.

As the ball begins the downward arc let the left hand drop from the ball at approximately the same time you take the second step on the left foot. The second step should be slightly longer than the first. At this point the ball should be closely alongside your right leg. If it is not in this position, you either have failed to remove your left hand from the ball soon enough or you may have released it too soon. In either case you will probably find that the ball is ahead of your slide or that you are ahead of the ball at the foul line.

As the ball swings on back and up toward the 180° or half-way point of the swinging arc, the third step is taken on the right foot. This step is again slightly longer than the previous step. The height of the backswing may vary. The normal apex of the backswing is usually about the same height in the swinging arc as your starting point on the push away. Swing as far back as you can comfortably control, keeping your shoulders facing the target. Women in particular may not have the strength and therefore the control for a high backswing and should just let the ball swing naturally as far back as is comfortable and safe. Increasing the forward lean of the body from the hips on the second and third steps will result in a longer backswing. From this adjustment the arm muscles are assisted by more of the shoulder and back muscles. As a result the body is in a more mechanically efficient position, thus allowing the bowler with a weaker arm to obtain the additional ball speed that results from a longer backswing.

The third step is the most awkward for novice bowlers in that the right leg is forward and the right arm is back, a coordination which is in opposition to the more natural right-arm-back left-leg-forward pattern used in executing most sports skills. However, should you have difficulty with the third step, walk the pattern out slowly and practice it several times without the ball. *Remember*, on the backswing the arm should be in a "pendulum motion," swinging straight back close to the right side. Keep the shoulders and trunk facing the target. There is a possibility of a crooked backswing or overswinging if you allow the trunk to rotate to the right or drop your shoulder.

Figure 12—Third Step   *Figure 13—Fourth Step*

The fourth step is more of a slide than a step and is longer than the three previous steps. Execute the slide on the left foot simultaneously with the forward swing of the ball. The fourth step will vary in length with different bowlers, and should take the same amount of time as does the forward swing of the ball. Remember that three steps were involved with the first half of the arm swing pattern and only *one* slide step is taken for the second half of the arm swing prior to the release of the ball. The length of slide then actually depends on the speed with which the arm and ball swing forward. Don't be misled by this statement and attempt to rush the forward swing or forcefully "throw" the ball down the alley. You will not have the feeling of rushing to the foul line if you were "in time" on your previous steps, especially the first one. Still maintain the important thought of "rolling" the ball off the fingers and down the alley.

Evaluation Questions

Lean over and slowly roll a bowling ball along the floor to a partner. Can you feel the timing of the release of the fingers and thumb? Which comes out of the ball first for the hook delivery?

In sliding on the fourth step, slide with most of the weight on the ball of the foot. Bend the left knee and shift most of your body weight on to the sliding foot. This insures the "braking" action necessary to check the forward momentum of the body. The left foot should stop the sliding motion two to six inches from the line to keep you from fouling. Make sure your left foot is pointing straight ahead and your shoulders are facing the target.

As the ball swings forward to a point beyond the perpendicular or opposite and beyond the sliding foot, release it by letting it roll easily off the thumb and fingers in that order. The ball should contact the alley bed in front of the foul line. Have the feeling you are lifting the ball just over the line. To do this successfully, of course, the body and ball should reach the foul line at exactly the same time, and your arm should reach out toward the target and follow on through in an upward arc, elbow bending slightly as if reaching toward the ceiling. At the release or "explosion point," the right hand should still maintain its "shaking hands" position—thumb at ten o'clock and fingers at four o'clock. The standard hook delivery will automatically evolve if you concentrate on the foregoing techniques, the correct hand position, thumb slipping out of the ball first, and following straight through with an upward arc at the end of the swing. It is not necessary to force a hook by twisting the trunk, swinging the arm across in front of the body or turning the hand over.

Observe in Figure 13 the balanced follow-through position of the bowler at the foul line. The follow-through is as important to the bowler as it is to the baseball pitcher, the golfer, the javelin thrower, etc. Any

Can you identify the type of ball delivery shown in the diagram?

Evaluation Questions

TYPE OF DELIVERY

athlete projecting a ball or an object toward a target will attempt to guide that object in a direct line by maintaining contact with the object as long as possible for the desired angle of flight. A strong and well-balanced follow-through will also insure optimum speed of the ball. People who have insufficient strength tend to slow down on the forward arm swing motion even before the release of the ball with the result that the ball rolls very slowly and is apt to deviate more on its way to the pins.

Study Figure 13 once again and review these most important "check points" of the fourth step and follow-through position:

1. Weight on the left foot
2. Left knee bent
3. Left foot a few inches from the foul line and pointing toward your target
4. Right leg extended behind the body for balance
5. Left arm extended to the side to aid in balance
6. Shoulders facing the target
7. Body leaning forward at the line so that toe, knee, and shoulders form a vertical line
8. Right arm extended forward and upward
9. Eyes focusing on the target or spot

Most expert bowlers will "pose" or hold this delivery position until well after the ball has been released to insure proper balance and position during the ball release. This is a "must" for control, consistency, and high scores. All learners should set a goal for themselves and exaggerate the follow-through by attempting to pose for three counts after release, or until the ball is over a certain spot on the alley, or until the ball hits

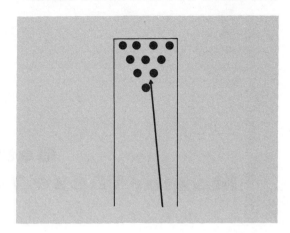

Diagram B:

TYPE OF DELIVERY

the pins. Maintaining a well-balanced delivery position after releasing a heavy ball is probably the most difficult of all the bowling techniques. Concentrate on perfecting it in every ball you roll.

Most of your success in bowling will depend on how you perform *behind* the foul line. When the ball isn't rolling to suit you, go back and check each of the fundamentals—the stance, the approach, the delivery and the follow through; better still, have an instructor or an expert bowler check them for you.

Straight Ball Delivery--For students who have difficulties controlling the hook, or for students who lack strength in the hands and wrists, the straight ball may prove more successful.

The fundamentals for delivering a straight ball (see Figure 9) are the same as for the hook. The differences are in the grip of the ball at the start and hand position at release.

Hold the ball in the starting position in exactly the same manner in front of the body as you would for the hook but rotate the ball so that the location of the thumb hole is at the twelve o'clock position. The finger holes are at approximately six o'clock. This grip allows more of the hand to be under the ball, providing some additional support as the ball is swung. The same "thumb on top" grip is also in effect as the ball is released at the foul line; however, the fingers slide out of the holes before the thumb. This is the reverse of the hook release.

The straight ball will have no spin; it should be released near the right gutter and roll on a diagonal line from right to left into the 1-3 pocket. The term "straight" means the absence of a hook or curve but the ball should not be rolled down the middle of the alley.

3

Better Players
Master These Techniques

It may be difficult for you to determine just when you should classify yourself as a "better player." Some beginners endowed with great natural ability may reach this category in relatively few lessons or practices while others may take one or two years to master the fundamentals. In addition to the amount of natural ability you possess are the factors of desire, motivation and your ultimate objective for learning the game. Do you want to learn just enough to "have fun with the gang" or do you really want to perfect each of the basic skills, learn the fine points of the game, and become an accomplished bowler? If your intent is toward the latter objective then you should allow plenty of time for instruction and buckle down to a good deal of practice. You should feel satisfied with each stage of your performance, and particularly with what goes on behind the foul line, before you tackle the fine points of the game. On the other hand bowling is not such a complicated sport to learn that the person with average skill can't "have fun" and knock down some pins after only a few lessons and a little practice. He may never get out of the "120" class in this "short-cut" program but a couple of strikes and spares per line can give him the enjoyment, recreation and exercise he wants or needs.

In either case, or for a person falling in the middle category between the two, the bowler should first be able to move his body and the ball "in time" up to the foul line, release the ball smoothly, and maintain balanced control of the body behind the foul line. Once the basic movement patterns have been learned and have become automatic, the ball control, accuracy, and consistency can be improved. This does not imply that you must be an experienced bowler before working on accuracy and consistency in where the ball goes. These are also very important in learning the game. A "better bowler" does not need to think about what he is going to do with his body in delivering the ball. He can concentrate on improving his aim, being more scientific in picking up spares, putting more "stuff" or spin on the ball, or studying more of the strategy of competitive bowling. Aiming and picking up spares are important parts of learning the game, but these techniques are not considered fundamental. A student by instinct or by trial and error could arrive at some method of aiming or picking up the remaining pins, but to become an average or accomplished bowler, he should learn a more scientific and effective method.

METHODS OF AIMING

There are three common methods of aiming the ball to get maximum pin fall. They are pin bowling, spot bowling and a combination of the two, line bowling. Each will be described and you may wish to experiment with all three before choosing one. However, if you wish to save some time and rely on statistics and recommendations of the experts, select the spot method. Almost all of today's top bowlers use this method. It is recommended for beginning bowlers mainly because the target (spot) is only 16 feet away as compared to one 60 feet away if the pins are used as a point of aim. It has also been found to be a more accurate and scientific method of picking up spares, correcting faults, or making allowances for variations in lane conditions.

The line method is the next most common method used. In it the bowler pictures an imaginary line painted on the lane over which his ball will travel. He also makes use of several check points along this line and concentrates on these as the ball progresses down the lane.

The least desirable point of aim is the pins because of their distance from the delivery point. Individuals who are extremely farsighted may have better results with this method, but it is not generally recommended.

Whatever system you choose, remember that bowling is based on a system of angles. For the proper chain reaction which will result in a strike, the ball contacts certain pins, then other pins hit against each other and are toppled. The standard hook ball must "drive" into the 1-3 pocket, breaking from right to left, and make a solid hit on the five pin. You should select whichever system of aiming will enable you to accomplish the strike most consistently.

Pin Bowling—By definition, this is the term for aiming directly at the pins. The pins, in general, cover a rather large area. Since the objective

23

Figure 14—Check Points for Spot Bowling

is to hit the 1-3 pocket, most pin bowlers will use the dark space between the one and three pins as the specific point of aim. They should also select a starting position on the right side of the approach and walk in the direction of the 1-3 pocket to insure the ball's coming into the pocket on the right to left angle. Many novice bowlers start out pin bowling because this is all they see or know. They erroneously bowl from the middle of the alley and aim at the head pin. Another disadvantage to pin bowling is the inclination for the bowler to follow through incorrectly or pull up too soon. The focus should be at the base of the pins to aid him in staying down on the follow-through.

Spot Bowling—In this method, which is strongly recommended, you, the bowler, focus your eyes on a designated spot or board in the alley about 16 feet from the foul line. You do not look at the pins until the ball has crossed over your spot or target. This idea may seem strange at first because you are trying to hit the 1-3 pocket without looking at it, but it works. You also plan to arrive at the foul line so that your right shoulder is in line with the spot. This enables your arm to follow straight through toward the spot so that the ball, when released, will roll over this target. Actually a good spot bowler uses several other spots as check points to make sure on his approach that he stays in line with the "spot" out on the alley. The spots indicated in Figure 14 are used for the strike ball.

This diagram shows the check points used by a bowler with an average hook ball. Once you have a consistent hook ball you will need to experiment with your check points. If your ball hooks more than this you should pick a spot (D) one or two boards right of the second arrow; if it hooks less, then try one or two boards left. You also can move your starting position one or two boards right or left to give you more or less angle going in to the pins.

THE STARTING POSITION. Before you make your four step approach, look down at your feet and see if they are placed in exactly the same position for every first ball you bowl. The first set of dots at the rear of the alley is 15 feet from the foul line and is used by most men or tall women with a long stride. The second set of dots is 12 feet from the foul line and should be used by persons with a shorter stride. Be specific and see that either the toes or heel of your right or left foot are in a certain location relative to one of the dots. Also make sure your starting position is to the right of center for your hook to break from right to left into the pocket.

Notice that the foot position at "A" is slightly left of the second check point, "B." This allows for the right shoulder to be over "B" at the release point.

THE RELEASE OR FOOTWORK CHECKPOINT. Your release point ("B") is actually beyond the foul line but your hand and ball should swing over the second dot or in close proximity to it. The "B" check point also helps you to walk a straight path to the foul line during your four-step approach. Take a quick glance at the second dot as you go into your approach because you obviously cannot look down to check it as you release the ball. If you have a tendency to "drift" or walk to the left in the approach, have someone sit directly behind you and watch to see how far left of the second dot you deliver the ball. An even better method of correcting a crooked approach is to check your left foot position in relation to the dots at the foul line. If you are walking straight up to the line your left foot should stop just short of approximately the third dot from the right and your left foot should point straight ahead. Of course you must maintain your balance at the foul line in order to be able to check the left foot position at "B."

ANGLE SPOTS. These are seven feet beyond the foul line and may be used to check the angle your ball is taking. Some nearsighted bowlers

How is your concentration? After delivering a ball can you tell by how many boards, if any, you missed your spot?

Evaluation Questions

prefer to use one of these as "the spot" or point of aim instead of the usual "D" spot.

POINT OF AIM. This is the all important "spot" in the spot bowling technique. Actually it is not a spot but a brown arrow or dart built into the alley. The seven arrows are called the "range finder" and help you to find your range on both strikes and spares. You must keep your eyes glued on this spot as you approach, release and follow through. Watch the center of the ball roll over the spot. There is a great temptation to look up too soon to see if you get your strike.

One of the chief advantages of the spot method is that if you're really watching the ball in relation to the "D" spot, you can compensate your aim. Suppose you have rolled three balls in a row which have hit the head pin and left you with splits. You then have a choice of shifting your point of aim one or two boards right of your original spot or of moving your starting position slightly to the left, using your same spot. Either move will have the same corrective effect. Do not be too hasty in changing your spot. Wait until a repeated error develops.

THE 1-3 POCKET OR STRIKE POCKET. If all four previous spots have "checked out," you should end up with a 1-3 pocket hit. This may happen and yet for some reason you don't get a strike. There is a point of accuracy even within the pocket and, depending upon which pins are left standing, you usually can analyze what went wrong. It takes a while to determine which niche in the pocket is right for your ball. In general, if you are leaving splits or corner pins, you're in the pocket but the ball is hitting too squarely on the head pin. If you leave the five or center pins you are usually too light on the head pin.

Should you miss "E" completely but hit all other check points, your trouble could be in the ball release. Your approach and follow-through may have been straight to the spot but you may have turned your wrist too much right or left or have released the fingers prior to the thumb, causing the ball to go straight instead of hook. Additional tips for improvement can be found in Chapter 4.

Line Bowling—The line bowling system is a combination of spot and pin bowling. The bowler who line bowls usually imagines a black line painted on the lane which runs from the range fingers or a spot on the alley to the pins. This line approximates the path his ball should take. This system is often more desirable than pin bowling for the hook bowler because he "sees" the curved line hooking into the 1-3 pocket.

PICKING UP SPARES

Your ability to pick up spares (knock down the pins remaining after bowling your first ball) can make the difference in whether you become a low or a high average bowler. Too often beginning bowlers are so engrossed in the idea of getting strikes that when they miss on the first ball, they hurry the process of rolling the second ball and throw it carelessly at the remaining pins so they can quickly get at the next full set of pins. Calculate for a minute the possibility of your rolling a 180 or 190 game without even making a strike. You merely have to be accurate in converting a one or two pin leave in each frame into a spare.

Of course the object of bowling is to knock down as many pins as you can on the first ball. If you first ball is too far off the mark you are going to leave pins standing that will be difficult for you to knock down for a spare. But comparatively speaking, there are very few leaves that cannot be spilled from the alley by a well-placed second ball. With the proper know-how and practice on various spare angles, the average bowler can learn to clear the alley at least 90 per cent of the time. The other 10 per cent of the time may find him faced with "impossible" splits. The good bowler knows that he must calculate, rolling his second ball very carefully to make sure that the one or two "key" pins struck by the ball are hit in such a manner that they will knock any other pins off the alley. How is this done?

First of all, keep consistent the delivery style on your second ball that you use on your first ball. Make as few adjustments as are absolutely

*Figure 15—Three Basic Spare
Angles*

necessary; those should be mainly in the starting position or in the point of aim. The type of ball you roll should remain the same, that is, if you roll a hook, stick with the hook on each ball. Some spares may appear rather impossible to get with a hook but it can be done. Do not switch to a straight ball on your second ball, not even on difficult leaves.

Likewise your method of aiming should remain the same on both balls. If you spot bowled the first ball then do so on the second. Many beginners who learn to spot bowl on the first ball decide to look at the pins on the second ball because it is simpler and less time-consuming than figuring out a new spot or adjusting the starting position so many boards right or left. Actually the adjustments are not that difficult to determine once the concept of the three basic spare angles is understood; they are the middle spare (5) left side spare (7), and the right side spare (10).

As a general plan in converting left and right side spares, angle the ball across the lane at the remaining pins. This gives you maximum lane surface over which to roll the ball. Observe in the diagram that the main adjustments occur in the position of the feet at the beginning of the approach, the dot over which you release the ball at the foul line, and your spot for aiming. With this system of picking up spares, the second and third arrows or somewhere in between the two are the only targets needed. You may need to deviate one or two boards, depending on the lane conditions and the extent of your hook.

Take time to figure out the best angle for converting a particular spare, contemplate which pins the ball will get and which pin(s) will topple other pins. In your early days of learning watch other bowlers attempting to pick up spares and notice how the ball deflects when it hits the pins. It angles quite sharply right or left depending on the approach angle, the number of pins it is contacting and whether it hits the right or left side of the pins. It does not continue on a direct path straight through the pins. Note the right and left deflections in Figure 16.

Occasionally you may observe a bowler, even an expert, who will roll a straight ball at the right side spares or who moves his starting position and his spot a few boards left for left side spares. This is done especially if the 2-pin is involved in order to narrow the angle and prevent a "cherry pick" or "chop" in certain situations. This is called "covering" your spare.

Here are a few examples of some rather common leaves with suggestions as to best ways of converting them into spares. One general rule, if all else is forgotten, is to plan on hitting the pin closest to you to get your spare.

Light Hit—1-3 Pocket   *Brooklyn Hit—1-2 Pocket*
Right Deviation   *Left Deviation*

Figure 16—Ball Deflections—Right, Left

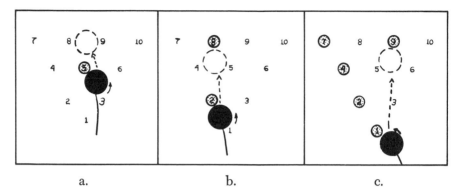

a.   b.   c.

Figure 17—Middle Spares

MIDDLE SPARES—STRIKE BALL POSITION

Figure 17a. The 5 or "king pin" is usually left up because of a light hit on the head pin.

Try your strike ball again, making sure you concentrate on your spot. A single pin in the center of the lane is one of the easiest spares to get. You have a 23" target—combined width of 2 balls (9" width) and the pin (4¾" width).

Figure 17b. This leave is called a "sleeper" and is a difficult one to spare without "cherrying." To prevent this, you must hit the 2 pin quite solidly. For a right-handed hook bowler, this can be done by shooting a strike ball if you move your feet and your spot about two boards left, giving you less angle and decreasing your chances of picking off the 2 only. The ball hits the 2, the 2 kicks off to the left and the ball goes back on a slightly right deflection and gets the 8.

Figure 17c. This is a deceptive leave for the inexperienced bowler. On first glance it appears that a head pin or 1-2 pocket hit down the middle would be the answer. With these hits you undoubtedly would leave up the 9. Here is where ball deflection is of prime consideration. If the ball hits left of the head pin, it will deflect left after the hit—the 1, 2, 4, & 7 will go down but the 9 will remain. A strike ball hitting the right side of the 1 will cause a chain reaction of the 1, 2, 4, & 7, and the ball will deflect right and go back and take out the 9.

LEFT SIDE SPARES

These include leaves on the left side of the lane with the ball being delivered from the right side.

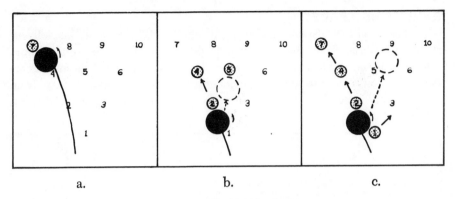

Figure 18—Left Side Spares

Figure 18a. Begin the approach about five boards or one dot right of your usual starting position to give you the widest angle and the most alley surface. Face toward the 7 pin and walk in that direction on your approach. Release the ball between the first and second dot and spot the second arrow or one or two boards left of it, depending on the extent of your hook. Do not "loaf" or ease up on the delivery because the ball must carry the hook to the last row of pins. The tendency is to get too much angle and roll into the gutter before reaching the pin. Remember there is more room on the right of the 7 pin than on the left.

Figure 18b. This spare results from a very thin hit on the right of the head pin. It is easy to "pick" either the 4 or 5 pin so you must come into the 2-5 pocket strong enough to cause the 2 to take out the 4 and the ball will deflect slightly right to go back and get the 5 pin.

Even if you pull your ball left you may still hit the 2-4 pocket and the 2 pin will get the 5 pin.

Assume your strike ball position and bowl between the second and third arrows for a Brooklyn hit.

Figure 18c. Here is a case of the ball not hooking and missing the head pin. The safest play is a 1-2 pocket ball because the ball contacting the 2 will cause the chain reaction of the 2 hitting the 4 and the 4 hitting the 7.

Use your far right starting position from the first dot and aim for the second arrow. The 1-2 pocket is not as far left as the 7 pin, therefore your right to left angle need not be as great.

This spare can be converted with a well-aimed strike ball but this is risky. If your strike ball is a little wide you miss all the pins, whereas if you pull the 1-2 pocket ball you may get 2 or 3 pins anyway.

RIGHT SIDE SPARES

These include "leaves" on the right side of the lane and the delivery should be made from the left side. Right side spares are usually more difficult for the right-hander to convert. The occasions when he must bowl from the left side are not as frequent and his ball hooks away from right to left instead of hooking into the pins as is the case in the left side spares.

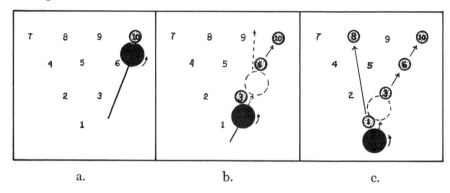

a.   b.   c.

Figure 19—Right Side Spares

Figure 19a. A very difficult single pin to pick up because it is sitting just 2½″ from the gutter.

Start from the extreme left, feet near the far left dot. Face the pin and walk toward it. Release the ball between the third and middle dots from the left and aim at the third arrow from the right. Be sure you follow through strongly. If you give up too soon you will pull the ball left and miss.

Beginners tend to get too much angle and go into the right gutter, so try aiming one board left of the third arrow if you have this difficulty.

Figure 19b. Again start in the far left position and walk toward the pins. You want the ball to hit the right half of the 3 pin so you won't need quite as sharp an angle as for the 10 pin alone. Aim for a point between the third and middle arrow from the right.

Hitting the right half of the 3 will send the 6 pin against the 10.

Figure 19c. This spare is more of a right center spare than a far right spare like the 3-6-10. It requires slightly less angle and a head pin hit or slightly high on the head pin so that the head pin will fly back and get the 8; the ball then gets the 3-6-10. Start left of center and aim for the center arrow or one or two boards right of the center, depending on the amount of hook on the ball.

SPLITS

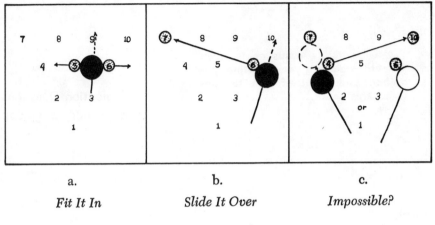

a.	b.	c.
Fit It In	*Slide It Over*	*Impossible?*

Figure 20—Splits

A split is a "leave" of two or more pins with the head pin down and a gap of at least one pin between any other two pins. A split occurs when your first ball hits too "heavy" or "high" on the head pin.

Figure 20a. "Fit Ins" are so called because the ball must be accurately placed between the two pins to convert the spare. Actually there are only about two inches more in ball width than the distance between the two pins. Your angle must be accurate so the ball will hit both pins.

Bowl this from a starting position about one dot left of center, spotting the third arrow. This is a right center spare and will not require as much angle as a 10 pin spare.

Figure 20b. The 7 pin is a row behind the 6 pin; consequently the ball must hit the 6 pin not only on the right side to slide it over but must hit toward the front right side to slide it over at the proper angle. Bowl from the left side and spot for the 10 pin position so the ball will hit thinly on the 6 pin.

Figure 20c. It is practically impossible to get all four pins unless one pin flies back into the kickbacks and rebounds onto the alley to take out the remaining pin in the split. Try for two or even three pins. From your experience decide whether the 4-7-10 or 6-7-10 is easier and pretend you have just three pins remaining. The ball will contact the two corner pins, the 6-10 and the 6 will slide over and take out the 7. Aim for either the 10 pin or 7 pin hit so the 6 or 4 will be hit thin and slide over.

Describe the adjustments you would make in your starting position and point of aim to convert this spare.

Evaluation Questions

CONVERTING A SPARE

TAPS

A tap is the chief lament of the better bowler because it seems to be a solid pocket hit but for some strange reason one pin is left standing. For the right-hander the most common tap is the 10 pin, others are the 8, 9, 7 and 4. Other single pin leaves are not usually the result of solid pocket hits. Taps are an unlucky part of the game and must be taken in stride. They are not due to the ball action but to one pin flying around another pin instead of taking it out. There is no remedy except positive thinking!

INFORMATION FOR ADVANCED STUDENTS OF THE GAME

Types of Ball Roll—For the average "once a week or less" bowler, the standard hook or straight ball is adequate. Most experts will agree that unless you are doing a great deal of competitive bowling two or three nights a week plus several hours practice a week, you should not attempt a "fancy" delivery that you can't control. However if your ball lacks action or "stuff" so that you're getting very few strikes you may want to experiment with or get some instruction in learning to roll a different type of ball. You might also try out a finger tip or semi-finger tip ball to aid you in more lift at release. If you do attempt a change in style or type of ball roll, you must be prepared to face a drop in average temporarily while you erase the old habit patterns and build new ones.

SEMI-ROLLER OR THREE QUARTER ROLLER. The most popular of the hook balls is the semi-roller and the one that has been discussed throughout this book. It is probably the strongest of the hook balls but it is the

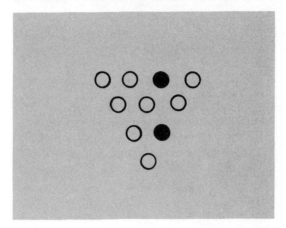

Diagram C:

CONVERTING A SPARE

timing of the release with the lift which determines the effectiveness of the hook. The semi-roller rolls on a track (the surface of the ball which contacts the lane) anywhere from one-half to three quarters of the ball's circumference. The ball should roll somewhere below the thumb hole to about two inches outside the thumb hole. The narrower the track on your ball the more consistent you are in rolling it. A ball rolling over the thumb hole sounds lopsided and loses "stuff" every time. This results from turning the wrist so that the thumb is down at release.

To effect a semi-roller all you need to do in addition to your regular hook ball grip is to lift the wrist upward and inward so the wrist is in a slightly cocked or flexed position at release. The fingers apply the lift (from the four o'clock position) moving upward and following the outward contour of the ball to about the two o'clock position at the time of release.

Full Roller. The full roller is delivered much like the straight ball except for the position of the thumb and fingers at release. Instead of the fingers letting go from behind the ball (five o'clock position) on the straight ball delivery, they release from the side of the ball at about the three o'clock position. The lift is straight up with no broken or cocked wrist position as in the semi-roller. It rolls on its full axis with the track not over an inch in width and appearing between the thumb and finger holes.

Semi-spinner. For bowlers who feel a natural inclination to roll or turn the wrist at release the semi-spinner may be an effective type ball. The regular hook ball grip is used but at the explosion point in the release

35

Describe the adjustments you would make in your starting position and point of aim to convert this spare.

Evaluation Questions

CONVERTING A SPARE

the wrist turns counterclockwise so that the fingers are at about two o'clock and the thumb at eight. There is also some finger lift at release. The track for the semi-spinner is wider and cone-shaped.

FULL SPINNER. This is a weak type of hook and is not recommended, particularly on fast lanes. It is released with little or no finger lift and with the wrist turning counterclockwise from a thumb on top position to a finger on top position. This puts terrific spin on the ball but it is difficult to control under varying lane conditions.

BACK UP. This is another type of delivery that is not recommended because of the unnatural hand position at release and the troubles with control. It is being described only for those (particularly women with weak wrists and hands) who start to develop a back up so that they will recognize it immediately and do something about it. A back up may develop when a person learning to roll a straight ball attempts to put more speed on the ball. She may twist the wrist clockwise so the thumb is at the one o'clock position at release and comes out of the ball after the fingers. The ball fades to the right, breaking away from the 1-3 pocket so the back up bowler usually aims for the 1-2 pocket and bowls from the left of center on the approach. This is the least desirable type of ball roll and angle.

Ball Action—If you closely examine a hook or curve ball rolling down the lane you will notice that the average ball skids about fifteen feet (to your spot), then rolls the next twenty feet and finally turns for the last twenty feet. At the beginning of the final twenty feet or turn, the spin motion is overcoming the forward motion of the ball. For this reason the

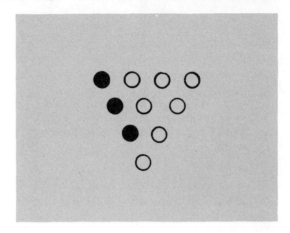

Diagram D:

CONVERTING A SPARE

ultra fast ball is ineffective. It skids farther, rolls less and hooks very slightly, thus giving little opportunity for the pins to mix.

With a curve which is a much slower delivery (but more difficult to control), the ball does not skid so much and the roll turns into a curve sooner taking more spin at the finish. If your curve quits on you, it is because it has started to hook too soon and you need to throw the ball out more on the alley.

Lane Conditions—No two bowling lanes are the same. Each pine board may have a different amount of pitch and it is the pitch that slows up the ball. A reddish colored board will have more pitch in it than a yellowish colored board, and it will "take" to the spin of the ball, thus producing a more decided hook. This is called a "running" alley. A "holding alley" is one which is faster, holds down the action of the hook, and the hook will not break as much. With the new lacquer being used on the lanes, it is very difficult to see where the balls have worn a track. There is a very thin oil dressing (only two ounces on an entire bed) so only an expert can detect the track. The only way you can tell what the alley will do to your ball is bowl on it.

To adjust to alley conditions you must move to the right or left of your starting angle according to how the alley affects your usual delivery. If your ball is not "finishing," that is missing the head pin on the right, then move slightly to your right to get a sharper angle. The reverse is true if you are pulling the ball into the 1-2 pocket. Move your starting position to the left. Watch that you do not move so far left that your body is to the left of the headpin, for this is a difficult angle from which to make strikes because of the deflection of the ball.

37

If a lane is said to be fast, would you be apt to change your spot to the right or left of your usual mark?

Evaluation Questions

Bowling Strategy—As in other sports, the strategy of the game depends on the situation. If you are bowling an important team match where each pin down is vital, you may use a different strategy than you would in an informal game with friends. In the latter situation where your performance affects only yourself, you may take many more chances in converting difficult splits than you would if your team were depending on you.

One of the first things you can do is to study the tournament temperament and how the various individuals on the opposing team react to pressure. Some bowlers thrive on competition; others get to a point where they cannot relax. Some are great front runners and are terrific as long as they are in the lead, but as soon as someone catches up with them, they fall apart. Others get better under pressure and have to get behind to throw a relaxed ball. These are the strong finishers. Study the psychological strategy first; some later decisions may depend on how well you know your opponents.

Another important part of bowling strategy is making decisions on how to bowl against splits. If you happen to draw a split (or even a large cluster of pins) after a strike, be certain to "count" down as many pins as possible because each extra pin down counts as two in the scoring. Always be very careful after a strike and do your best to strike again or at least hit the pocket and get a big count.

In most situations after a split occurs, play it safe and attempt to get one pin of two or two of three. If you are the last man and the game or match depends on your conversion, then of course you must try it. Many a game is won or lost by a pin or two. Never try to convert the "railroads" (7-10, 4-6, 7-9 etc.) by sliding one pin into another. Your chances are very remote and you will often miss both pins by trying to hit one lightly on the side. Again if you need to "go for broke" in this situation, your chances are better if you roll the ball into one pin solidly and slam it into the cushion and hope it will fly back into the other pin.

Understand the importance of the "ninth frame" strategy. Try your best to strike in the ninth so you can lay a foundation and develop a relaxed feeling for your tenth frame. Remember with two extra balls it is possible to "turkey out" in the tenth. One last bit of advice, yet one of the keys for team success, is for you to be "strategic" with yourself. Relax, concentrate, take "the bitter with the better" and work toward being a dependable, consistent bowler. You are much more valuable to your team with these attributes than if you are an erratic, temperamental individual who bowls 220 one game and 120 the next.

Progress
Can Be Speeded Up

By now you should have an understanding of what achievements are necessary to become an accomplished bowler. The methods you choose for progressing rapidly toward these achievements are likewise important. Obviously the best method is a program of instruction and guided practice with a qualified bowling instructor. The next best thing would be a few lessons on the fundamentals of delivery, some additional reading, study, and observation of what the experts recommend, and then a great deal of self-directed practice. A periodic check by your original instructor will save you time and effort in undoing the wrong habit patterns which develop so quickly.

CONDITIONING AND WARMUPS

Although bowling is not as rigorous as many other sports, the swinging of a 12-16 pound weight on the end of your arm for any period of time can be fatiguing to the unconditioned. Before starting out on a "training program" for becoming an accomplished bowler, make sure you have adequate strength in your right hand and arm and a sturdy left leg. These exercises are recommended primarily for women bowlers who may lack initial strength.

Improving Grip Strength

1. Squeeze a small rubber ball (handball size) in the palm of your right hand. Hold the hand in the regular hook position, relax the thumb and squeeze the ball with the second and third fingers about twenty times twice a day.

Dropping Ball

Poor Balance

Compensation

Sidewheeling

Drifting to Left

Drifting to Right

Figure 21—Common Faults

Can you pick off the 10 pin from a full rack of pins without knocking down any other pin?

Evaluation Questions

2. Practice swinging a heavier bowling ball than you ordinarily use. While you're waiting your turn to bowl, move to the back of the seats or an uncongested walkway and swing the ball continuously back and forth until your arm is fatigued. Use your regular hook grip and keep this grip throughout the swing process. Try to increase the number of swings each day you do the exercise.

Strengthening the Left Leg—Walking and going up and down stairs keeps your legs in good enough condition for the amount of bowling done by the average bowler. For beginning bowlers, however, merely balancing on the left foot, knee bent, left arm extended sideward, right arm extended forward in the normal follow-through position is not only a good exercise for the thigh muscles but will help improve your balance.

SPECIFIC AIDS FOR COMMON FAULTS

Probably the two most common errors made by all inexperienced bowlers are improper timing of the steps and arm swing on the approach and poor balance and follow-through at the foul line.

By using the one simple remedy of slowing down the approach you may avoid one or more of the following errors: (1) forcing the ball, (2) bouncing it, (3) dropping it, (4) drifting, (5) fouling, slipping or sticking at the foul line, or (6) delivering a ball that fails to come into the pocket but stays to the right of the pocket. The easiest way to slow down the approach is to shorten the first step (and possibly the second and third), shorten the push away and start it simultaneously with the first step, and most important of all, think of rolling the ball smoothly as you progress toward the foul line.

If you have attempted to slow down your approach but your balance and follow-through are still poor, check the following remedies: (1) On the fourth step slide with the weight forward on the ball of the left foot, just as you would if you were sliding on ice; (2) bend the left knee as you slide and shift most of the body weight to the left foot, lowering the heel as you slide to act as a brake in stopping forward momentum; (3) extend your left arm out to the side to counterbalance the release of the weight (ball) from your right side; (4) keep your left foot pointing straight ahead and shoulders facing your target or spot, and (5) lean forward and reach strongly straight out toward your spot after the ball has been released.

OTHER COMMON FAULTS AND THEIR REMEDIES

Improper Arm Swing Pattern

1. *Too high a backswing* leads to loss of control and perhaps too much speed for a good working ball.

    Remedy: Do not allow your trunk to rotate to the right ("side-wheeling") on the backswing. Keep your shoulders facing the target and allow the ball to swing back to a comfortable height and straight back in line with the target.

2. *Too low a backswing*, common among women bowlers, usually means a loss of sufficient speed on the ball. This plus the lighter ball used by women bowlers makes it difficult to get many strikes.

    Remedy: The first thing to do is to strengthen the grip if you are swinging short for fear of dropping the ball. Move the ball to a higher starting position under the chin, thus allowing more time and a longer swinging arc to build up momentum for a longer backswing. Practice swinging the ball back naturally as far as it will go and after it has reached the apex of the arc, let gravity and the weight of the ball furnish the forward swing power.

3. *Crooked backswing* where the arm swings out too far from the body on the backswing or in too far behind the body the result is a diagonal forward swing in the opposite direction and the ball will go too far right or left of the mark.

    Remedy: Swing the ball straight back close to the right side toward an imaginary target behind you in line with your right shoulder. Keep your shoulders and trunk facing your target.

Then swing the ball straight forward toward your mark out on the alley.

Overturning or Turning the Ball Too Soon—This results in trying to put too much "stuff" on it so that you twist or jerk the ball at release.

Remedy: Let the ball do the work by letting your thumb and fingers slide out of the ball easily and smoothly. Make the release a flowing motion. Wait until the ball has passed your left foot on the forward swing before you break or lift the wrist. The weight of the ball may cause the wrist to turn slightly, but do not force a turn.

Missing Your Point of Aim—If your angle is bad or lane conditions are such that you are consistently missing your spot to the same side, try changing your starting position to allow for more or less angle.

1. *Consistently left* of your spot means too much angle or ball released too soon.

    Remedy: Move your starting position only a few boards left. Keep your same point of aim.

2. *Consistently right* of your spot means not enough angle or ball released too late.

    Remedy: Move your starting position a few boards to your right, keeping your original point of aim.

HINTS FOR LEARNING AND PRACTICE

In addition to good instruction and reading up on some of the fine points of the game, your learning can be enhanced by watching the experts. Watch their various styles of delivery on television or go to your nearest bowling establishment the night the scratch leagues are bowling, find out who the bowlers with the highest averages are and observe them closely. Sit directly behind them and concentrate on their straight line approach and follow-through, then move to a position where you have a side view of their timing of the steps and arm swing and their body position at the foul line. Concentrate on the bowlers themselves in action and not the pins going down. Also observe their methods for picking up spares and splits. As soon as the first ball is bowled and if pins remain, quickly analyze your procedure for the second ball and see if the bowler does what you would have done in the same situation. This mental practice can be used when bowling with friends or watching others bowl on adjacent lanes. How would you pick up those spares if you were doing it?

One of the best aids in learning a new activity is the motion picture. Study films of the experts, or have movies taken of your performance and compare it with those of the experts.

Practicing a great deal at the bowling alley may run into some expense and it may become difficult to discipline yourself to practice instead of bowling games. Typically, watching the pins fall down and scoring begin to take most of your attention and you neglect concentrating on fundamentals. Bowling without pins or "shadow bowling" is practically a must for proper learning of the fundamentals of the approach and delivery. Go to the lanes when they are not busy and pay your money to just roll the ball for an entire line. Do this as many times as is necessary to develop a smooth, rhythmical, mechanical delivery.

After this has been accomplished, bowl many lines without keeping score. Re-rack the pins each time and practice rolling your strike ball until you consistently hit your spot. When your strike ball is working well, shadow bowl at imaginary left and right side spares. It is very easy to tell whether or not your practice ball would have gotten the spare. With the pins up, try a line of bowling attempting to pick off just the 7 pin or just the 10 pin. The automatic pin machines make it difficult to practice spare bowling but you can practice your various spare angles to see if you're hitting your spot.

Dedicate yourself to a few hours practice by yourself so you can concentrate your full time on the task at hand. Once you start keeping score, make notes to yourself on the score sheet, particularly in regard to your spot. You may discover some objective evidence of first or second ball inconsistencies.

This book has attempted to give you a point of reference or a basis for building good bowling habits. Each bowler will develop his own style and methods for practice through discovering his best working pace. Discover it, stay with it and enjoy a fascinating game in the process.

5

The Language
and Lore of Bowling

"Bowl" is thought to be derived from the Saxon "bolla" and the Danish "bolle" both meaning, in the literal sense, bubble. The word later referred to any round or spherical object. Some authorities trace the word to the Latin "bulla" or round ball and others prefer the French derivation "boule" meaning ball.

Throwing, pitching or rolling objects at targets has for centuries been an innate urge in man, and the earliest records of such activity used as a game were discovered by an English Egyptologist, Sir Flinders Petrie. While examining the contents of an Egyptian child's grave, the burial date placed at 5200 B.C., he discovered implements and objects for playing a game very similar to our tenpins of today.

In other studies by Dr. Malcolm Rogers, curator of the San Diego museum, an ancient bowling game as performed by the Polynesians was found in which small elliptical balls and round, flat discs of stone, about 4 inches in diameter were used. The game was called Ula Maika and consisted of bowling or rolling the stones a distance of 60 feet, the same length of our hardwood lanes today.

Bowling's place of origin in Europe appears to have been in what is now Northern Italy, where as early as 50 B.C. the Helvetii played "Boccie," a game similar to the modern Italian bowling.

These ancient forms of bowling more closely resembled lawn bowling. Bowling at pins actually originated as a religious ceremony in the cloisters of cathedrals in Germany as early as the third or fourth centuries A.D. It was then the custom for the canons to test the faith of their parishioners by

46

having them place their pins at one end of the cloister and from the opposite end throw a ball at the pins which represented the "Heide" or heathen. If a hit was scored this meant the parishioner was leading a pure and clean life and would be able to slay the heathen; if he were unsuccessful at hitting the pins it meant that in order to improve his aim he would need to be more faithful in attendance at church services. Those who were successful were called "keglers" and were honored and toasted at a dinner given at the conclusion of the tests.

Figure 22—Early Egyptians Bowling (Courtesy of American Bowling Congress)

The game ceased to be a religious endeavor and developed into a sport when the canons became intrigued and began "kegling" with their cathedral students. The game changed to include as many pins as there were keglers.

47

What is the name of the hit shown in the diagram? What causes the ball to roll in this manner?

Evaluation Questions

SCORING

The first indoor bowling lanes are believed to have originated in England where, because of bad weather conditions, bowling on the open green was difficult. During the Middle Ages, to insure year around activity, the wealthy enthusiasts of the game constructed bowling annexes to their residences.

On the continent, bowling or ninepins soon became a universal pastime. In Germany, Martin Luther was an enthusiastic bowler and built a bowling lane for his family. The French had a game called Carreau which was played long before the reign of Charlemagne. The Dutch Pins version resembled skittles but with taller and narrower pins, especially the middle pin which was higher than the rest and called the king pin. Curling, another adaptation of the ancient game of bowls was introduced into Scotland by the Flemish in the sixteenth century. Bowling on ice became very popular in countries with severe winters.

In America, the early Dutch settlers brought the game of ninepins with them to Manhattan Island in 1626. Three citizens leased a plot which had been used for a parade ground or market place; this area was located at what is now the foot of Broadway in New York City. They enclosed it for a bowling green and the little park still bears its original name of Peppercorn.

Washington Irving in his "Rip Van Winkle" (1819) made one of the earliest references to pin bowling when he mentioned the thunder of the ball colliding with pins. The early game probably reached the height of popularity in the 1840's in New York where bowling lanes were found on nearly every block on Broadway and in various parts of the Bowery.

48

Diagram E:
HITTING TO THE LEFT

By 1850 gamblers and swindlers had complete control of the game of ninepins; most of the matches were rigged, and this led to the abolition of bowling in New York, Connecticut, and Massachusetts by a law in 1841 declaring it a gambling game.

Because of the great enthusiasm for the game unknown individuals in order to circumvent the law added one more pin, hence the origin of our present game of tenpins. It was allowed to grow and become well enough established so that by 1875 the "National Bowling Association" was formed to revise the rules and standardize the equipment. Although great credit is due this early association, it failed to make good and the American Amateur Bowling Union followed in 1890. It also disintegrated because of limitations and gave way to the American Bowling Congress whose purpose was to help promote and elevate the game. As a result of insight, purposeful planning and principles this organization is today the largest sports organization in the world, with a membership of more than 5,000,000 bowlers. The Women's International Bowling Congress was established in 1916, and the American Junior Bowling Congress, governing the instructions and competition of bowling for boys and girls, developed soon afterwards.

Bowling establishments are no longer thought of with ill respect and as an evil atmosphere for women and children. Today with the construction of large bowling centers containing 100 lanes or more, lounges, dining rooms, and even nurseries, bowling has lost its unsavory "pool hall" association and has become one of the largest participating sports and one of the most popular forms of family recreation in the United States.

BOWLER'S LINGO

Almost every sport has a language uniquely its own and bowling probably has one of the most colorful vocabularies of all. If you should bowl in various parts of the United States, you may need to learn a new terminology. Bowlers in Los Angeles and Chicago call a 1-2 pocket hit for right handers a "Brooklyn," whereas the Brooklynites call it a "Jersey." Most of the terminology listed here is widely used but space is left for you to insert other lingo peculiar to your locale.

Remember that to master all aspects of bowling you should "talk" a good game as well as demonstrate it.

Terms Relating to the Ball

Backup: Ball that curves to the right for a right-hand bowler.

Bridge: Distance between finger holes on the ball.

Brooklyn: Ball hitting to left of the headpin (1-2 pocket) for right-hand bowlers.

Creeper: A very slow ball.

Cross Over: Same as "Brooklyn."

Dead Ball: A poorly rolled ball which deflects off course.

Flat Apple or *Flat Ball*: Same as "dead ball."

Flat Apple

Gutter Ball: A poorly rolled ball which goes off the lane into the gutter before reaching the pins.

Hook: A ball that breaks to the left as it nears the pins for a right-hand bowler.

Loft: Throwing the ball too far out on the lane beyond the foul line.

Pitch: The angle at which the finger holes are bored in the ball.

Span: Distance between thumb and finger holes.

Sweeper: A good working ball that sweeps the pins off the lane.

Working Ball: A very effective hook ball with much action or spin.

Others

....

....

Terms Relating to the Bowler

A.B.C.: American Bowling Congress.

Anchor: A person bowling in fifth position on a team, usually the one with the highest average.

Choke: To tense under pressure.

Foul: Touching or going beyond the foul line as the ball is delivered.

Kegler: Another name for bowler.

W.I.B.C.: Women's International Bowling Congress.

Choke

Others

....

....

Terms Relating to the Lanes

Alley: Another name for lane.

Approach: The area on which the bowler takes his steps prior to delivering the ball at the foul line.

Foul Line: The line that separates the approach from the lane.

Graveyard: The lane or lanes which are toughest for a bowler to score on.

Graveyard

Kick Backs: The division or side boards at the pit end of the lane.

Lane Conditions:

Holding: A fast lane which cuts down on the amount of hook.

Return: The track on which the ball rolls back from the pit to the ball rack.

Rough, Tough, or *Mean*: Lanes which are difficult to score on.

Running: A slow lane which allows more hook.

Soft: Lanes which are easy for you to score on.

Spot: A certain place on the lane at which the bowler aims. Range finder.

Stiff: Same as fast or holding lane.

Others

....

....

51

Terms Relating to the Pins

Baby Split: The 2-7 or 3-10 splits.

Bedposts: The 7-10 split.

Big Four: The 4-6-7-10 split. Also known as "double pinochle."

Bucket: The 2-4-5-8 leave.

Cherry: Picking off the front pin of a spare and leaving other pins standing.

Bedposts

Headpin: The number one pin.

Kingpin: The number five pin.

Pocket: The space between the 1-3 pins for a right-hand bowler; space between the 1-2 pins for left-hand bowler.

Railroad: Synonym for split.

Sleeper: A pin hidden directly behind another pin.

Split: Two or more pins standing with intermediate pins knocked down in front and between.

Tap: Leaving a 10, 4, or 7 pin on what appeared to be a strike ball.

Washout: The 1-2-4-10 leave for a right-hander; the 1-3-6-7 leave for a left-hander.

Woolworth: The 5-10 split.

Others

....

....

Terms Relating to Scoring

Blind: Score given a team for an absent member.

Blow: An error. Failing to spare, except following a split.

Double: Two strikes in succession.

Dutchman: A 200 game consisting of alternating strikes and spares.

Frame: The box on the score sheet in which the score is registered; one-tenth of a game.

Handicap: A predetermined method of awarding extra points to an individual or team with a lower average.

Line: A game of ten frames.

Mark: Getting a strike or spare.

Open Frame: A frame without a strike or spare.

Scratch: Using actual scores without handicaps.

Spare: All pins knocked down on two balls.

Strike: All pins knocked down on the first ball.

Strike Out: Three successive strikes in the tenth frame, or striking to the finish of the game.

Turkey: Three strikes in a row.

Turkey

Others

....

....

Scoring and Rules
of the Game

A game or line of bowling for an individual consists of ten frames or ten attempts, rolling one or two balls, to knock down all ten pins in each frame. The game score is the total number of pins knocked down in the ten frames.

The symbols for scoring are marked in each frame as follows:

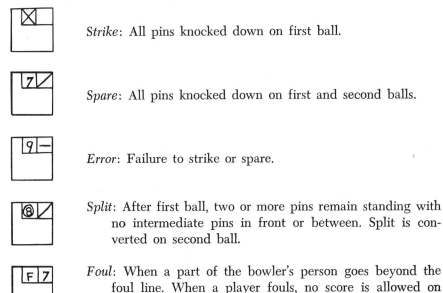

Strike: All pins knocked down on first ball.

Spare: All pins knocked down on first and second balls.

Error: Failure to strike or spare.

Split: After first ball, two or more pins remain standing with no intermediate pins in front or between. Split is converted on second ball.

Foul: When a part of the bowler's person goes beyond the foul line. When a player fouls, no score is allowed on that ball.

Evaluation Questions

Fill in the score in each frame for the line of bowling shown in the diagram.

6 /	7 2	X	X	X	9 -	F /	X	⑧ 1	9 / X	TOTAL
17	26	56	85	104	113	133	152	161	181	181

Actually scoring a game of bowling is quite simple if you follow **four** basic procedures:

1. *No strike or spare*—Merely add the total pins knocked down on **first** and second ball and score as follows: Scoring is accumulative.

2. *Strike*—Ten plus a bonus of the number of pins knocked down on the next two balls rolled.

3. *Spare*—Ten plus a bonus of the pins knocked down on the first ball of the next frame.

4. *Tenth Frame*—If a spare occurs in the tenth frame, the bowler is entitled to roll one more ball. If a strike occurs in the tenth frame, the bowler is entitled to two additional balls to finish his game.

HELPFUL HINTS

A combination of strike-spare or spare-strike in successive frames is always 20. Strike = 10 + next two balls. Spare = 10 + first ball in next frame.

A "double" or two strikes in a row is always twenty something (2-?) depending on the number of pins knocked down on the first ball rolled after the double, i.e., 10 + 10 + 8.

A triple or "turkey" scores 30 and is the highest figure which can be recorded or added on in any one frame, i.e., 10 + 10 + 10.

NOTE: This is how a perfect game of 300 can be scored (10 frames of 30 each).

The general playing rules for bowling are few and much less complicated than for most sports competition. The A.B.C. and W.I.B.C. are responsible for the rules and their interpretation. There are some technical rules involving the proper functioning of leagues which, because of lack of space, will not be listed here. They can be obtained by writing the A.B.C. or W.I.B.C. These are the important general rules:

OFFICIAL GAME[1]

The bowling of ten complete frames on a pair of lanes on which the game was started shall constitute an official game, unless equipment failure delays the normal progress of the game and in such cases the game or series may be finished on another pair of lanes.

The members of a team shall successively, and in regular order, bowl one frame on one lane, and for the next frame alternate and use the other lane, so alternating each frame until the game is completed.

In league play, the first game of a series shall be started on the lane on which a team is scheduled. Succeeding games shall be started on the lane on which a team has finished the preceding game.

Fouls

A foul is committed with no pinfall being credited to the player, although the ball counts as a ball rolled, when a part of the bowler's person encroaches upon or goes beyond the foul line and touches any part of the lane equipment or building during or after executing a legal delivery. A ball is in play and a foul may be called after legal delivery has been made and until the same or another player is on the approach in position to make a succeeding delivery.

---

[1]From the official rule book of the American Bowling Congress. Reprinted with permission.

Leagues must have a foul judge or an electric foul detecting device in operation. The captains of the opposing teams are responsible for the calling of fouls in the event of mechanical failure of the foul detecting device, and a foul judge is not available.

If a player deliberately fouls to benefit by the calling of a foul, he shall be immediately disqualified from further participation in the series then in play and his place is taken by another player. The deliberate foul shall not be allowed.

A player who wilfully throws his ball into the gutter shall be immediately removed from the game and series and his place may be taken by another player.

If no substitute is available, his team shall be credited only with the pins knocked down up to the time the player was disqualified plus one-tenth of his absentee score for each of the remaining frames in the game.

A foul ball shall be recorded as a ball bowled by the player, but any pins bowled down when a foul is committed shall not count. When a player fouls upon delivering the first ball of a frame, all pins knocked down must be respotted, and only those pins knocked down by the second ball may be counted. If all pins are bowled down with the second ball after fouling with the first, it shall be scored as a spare. A player who fouls when delivering the second ball of a frame shall be credited with only those pins knocked down on the first ball, provided no foul was committed on the first ball.

Pinfall

Legal—Every ball delivered by the player shall count, unless declared a dead ball. Pins must then be respotted after the cause for declaring such dead ball has been removed.

1. Pins which are knocked down by another pin or pins rebounding in play from the side partition or rear cushion are counted as pins down.

2. It is the player's responsibility to determine if the pin set up is correct. He shall insist that any pins incorrectly set be respotted before delivering his ball.

3. Pins which are knocked down by a fair ball, and remain lying on the lane or in the gutters are termed dead wood, counted as pins down, and must be removed before the next ball is bowled.

Illegal—When any of the following incidents occur, the ball counts as a ball rolled, but pins knocked down shall not count:

1. When pins are knocked down or displaced by a ball which leaves the lane before reaching the pins.
2. When a ball rebounds from the rear cushion.
3. When pins come in contact with the body, arms or legs of a pin setter and rebound.
4. A standing pin which falls upon removing dead wood or which is knocked down by a human pin setter or touched by mechanical pin setting equipment shall not count and must be replaced on the pin spot where it originally stood before delivery of the ball.
5. Pins which are bowled off the lane, rebound and remain standing on the lane must be counted as pins standing.

Dead Ball

A ball shall be declared dead if any of the following occur, in which case such ball shall not count. The pins must be respotted after the cause for declaring such dead ball has been removed and the player shall be required to rebowl:

1. If, after the player delivers his ball and attention is immediately called to the fact that one or more pins were missing from the set up.
2. When a player bowls on the wrong lane or out of turn.
3. When a player is interfered with by a pin setter, another bowler, spectator, or moving object as the ball is being delivered and before delivery is completed, the player must then and there accept the resulting pinfall or demand that pins be respotted.
4. When any pins at which the bowler is bowling are moved or knocked down in any manner, as the player delivers the ball and before it reaches the pins.
5. When a player's ball comes in contact with any foreign obstacle.

Replacement of Pins

Should a pin be broken or otherwise badly damaged during the game, it shall be replaced at once by another as nearly uniform in weight and condition as possible with the set in use.

A broken pin does not change the score made by a bowler.

Unwritten Laws

There is more than score to reflect how much a player knows about the game and how desirable he may be as a team member or bowling companion. He must behave like a true sportsman and show the common courtesies and respect to other bowlers on his team and on adjoining lanes that he wishes shown to him. Bowling etiquette is merely a demonstration of everyday politeness and of allowing other bowlers to concentrate fully on the task at hand.

A bowling center, because of its size, numbers of people bowling, and type of equipment, is a difficult atmosphere in which to concentrate; therefore, respect the wishes of the person on the lane and remain quiet until he has finished his turn. Do congratulate him and show enthusiasm for a job well done as pep and chatter at the proper time do wonders for the morale of the team. Know the personalities and temperaments of the people with whom you bowl. Some can take a lot of kidding or razzing while others may be insecure and need encouragement.

PRIORITY

Respect the bowler who is on the approach ready to make his delivery. Remain on the bench until it is your turn to bowl, then move promptly.

Wait until a bowler on the adjoining lane has delivered his ball before you step up to take your ball off the rack.

In general, give priority to the bowler on your right if he is ready to start his delivery at the same time you are. However, the bowler who has his spare to shoot has the right of way over the one who is rolling

Figure 23—Timely Tips on Bowling Etiquette. Distracting fellow bowler by lifting ball off rack at the wrong time.

his first ball unless he motions you to go ahead. He may wish to contemplate his spare a little longer.

There is an unwritten rule that if a bowler has a split left standing he will immediately take his second ball, so that the pins are cleared away. A bowler on an adjoining lane may not wish to see an awkward split staring him in the face when he is about to roll.

Between balls step to the rear of the approach or on to the floor behind the approach. The adjacent bowler may thus proceed without interference.

CONFINE "BODY-ENGLISH" TO YOUR OWN ALLEY

Keep your balance and control at all times. Limit your actions to the width of your own lane.

OBSERVE THE FOUL LINE

This goes for practice games as well as league play. Sliding carelessly beyond the foul line may develop into a habit that is difficult to break. If you foul frequently, try taking a shorter first step or move your starting position farther back.

SHOW CONSIDERATION FOR THE LANES AND EQUIPMENT

Replace house balls in their proper places on the rack after you have completed your bowling.

Check the number of your ball and use the same ball on the first and second attempts in a frame. Do not roll a different ball for your second roll. The machines (or pin boys) are timed to operate during the return of your original ball to the rack.

Refrain from blaming the equipment. The fault is probably yours and you should correct it.

Watch lofting the ball on your delivery. Use chalk or dry your hands if the ball is sticking. Lofting also may be due to poor timing on the release.

61

Show consideration for keeping the approaches clean by confining eating and drinking to the bench area and by making sure your bowling shoes are clean. Change to bowling shoes before stepping on the approaches.

Be sure the pin machine rack is up before you roll.

SHOW GOOD SPORTSMANSHIP AT ALL TIMES

Control your temper and your language. Constant complaints about bad luck or poor alley conditions are in bad taste, and you may become very unpopular as a bowling companion or teammate.

Refrain from giving advice unless you are asked for it. A bowler who is bowling badly may become more confused than ever. The best advice is "Take your time."

Watch your bragging. It is best to let your scores speak for you.

Accept defeat gracefully and congratulate your opponent or opponents for their good bowling.

KNOW THE PINS BY THEIR NUMBERS

This helps to speed up play, particularly if pins have been moved or knocked down accidently by the machines (or pin boy) and need to be respotted.

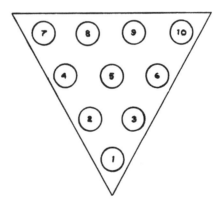

Figure 24—Learn Pins by Number

8

Facts for Enthusiasts

Once you have learned the fundamentals of bowling and have become enthusiastic about improving your scores and becoming a competent bowler, proper fitting personal equipment becomes a must. Rented or "house" balls and shoes are adequate for learning the game and up to the point where you have ceased experimenting with different weights, spans and types of balls, but as in any sport, the caliber and fit of your own equipment may help or hinder your performance. You will bowl much more consistently with your own ball and shoes.

A custom-fitted ball is also much less likely to cause blisters, swollen knuckles and perhaps even pulled muscles.

SELECTION AND PURCHASE OF A BALL

Weight—The selection of a "house ball" according to weight was discussed in Chapter 2. Before you purchase a ball, try out several house balls of different weights. Keep in mind that lighter balls which fit poorly may seem to weigh more than a heavier custom-fitted ball. In the learning stages it is best to start with a lighter ball until proper timing and control are perfected and then change to a heavier ball which, all things being equal, tends to get more pins down and stays "on line" better. Very few women bowlers can handle a 16 pound ball without dropping it or becoming excessively tired so a 12 or 14 pound ball is usually recommended. Some men of slight build or older men may do better with a load of 14 or 15 pounds.

Fitting—In having a ball drilled to fit your grip, be sure you deal with a reputable bowling manufacturer or custom driller who knows his

Figure 25—A Bowler's Personal Equipment

business. There are some measuring gadgets on the market that are not reliable. Remember that a poorly fitted 14 pound ball can feel heavier than a well fitted 16 pound ball.

Most dealers who sell balls employ an expert driller and the purchase of a ball will entitle you to custom fitting and drilling at no cost.

The question of the number of finger holes is debatable for men but most women should stick to the conventional three-fingered ball. The two-fingered ball and the "finger tip" ball require more strength, control and endurance. Many of the top performers today are using the "finger tip" ball but they usually bowl ten to twenty-five games a day and have developed excellent control and stamina. Make sure the thumb hole is drilled large enough to allow an easy release, and the finger holes fit more tightly to insure the proper release on a hook ball. If you bowl a straight or back up ball, this fact should be told to the driller. Also tell him if you are left-handed because the ring finger hole is usually drilled a fraction of an inch farther from the thumb hole than the second finger hole. This is the reason left-handers should not use right-handed balls.

The "pitch" in the bowling ball is also a very important part of the fit. "Pitch" refers to the degree of inclination the finger holes have toward or away from the center of the bowling ball.

The more the finger holes are cut in so that the fingers can approximate a more clenched position when they are inside the ball, the greater the grip feeling the bowler has. The standard for a conventional grip is ⅜" pitch above the center of the ball. Too much pitch can spoil the ability to release the fingers from the ball.

Balls can now be purchased in a variety of colors in addition to the traditional black. To appeal to the ladies' tastes, balls, shoes and ball bags can be purchased in matching colors and a variety of combinations.

Bowling gloves are also becoming quite popular and are recommended for persons who do a lot of competitive bowling, or who have soft or sensitive skin and develop blisters easily.

PURCHASE OF BOWLING SHOES

Comfortable and well fitted bowling shoes are another important item to consider for good performance in bowling.

For a right-handed bowler, the right bowling shoe should have a leather tip, rubber sole and heel. The left shoe should have a smooth leather sole for sliding and a rubber heel for "braking." A left-hander's shoes are made in the opposite fashion. There are many styles, colors and varieties of leather from which to choose.

BOWLING BAGS

Since bowling balls are quite heavy and awkward to carry, it is almost essential that you purchase a ball bag. A combination ball and shoe bag is even better. A bag also protects the ball from becoming scratched or nicked. They can be purchased in leather or imitation leather, canvas or a combination of materials. Make sure the handles are secured firmly because there is constant strain on them from lifting and supporting the heavy weight.

CLOTHES

Men usually have no problem about being comfortable and appropriately attired for bowling, but women should be warned again, as in Chapter 2, to wear skirts or dresses with enough width to allow the bending and sliding action necessary for a smooth delivery. The shirt or blouse should be loose in the shoulders in order to allow a free arm swing motion.

9

Playing the Game

Once you have learned the fundamental bowling techniques from a competent instructor and have practiced to the extent that you have a reasonable amount of consistency in the delivery of the ball, you may wish to try out your talents in a recreational or competitive situation. If you are not too sure of your own performance and wish to use scores as criteria for taking the initial dive into league competition, you would probably feel more at ease if you were capable of averaging 120 (women) or 140 (men). Recent studies of the performance of college bowlers at U.C.L.A. indicate that students with these or better averages are in the "intermediate" or "experienced" category, and thus most of them could enjoy league bowling. The studies also showed a difference of approximately 20 pins between averages of men and women in selected groupings of "beginning" and "experienced" bowlers.

Students in most of the larger colleges and universities have an excellent opportunity to learn bowling and to compete in intramural leagues right on their own campuses. The modern college student union buildings are including bowling lanes as part of the total campus recreation for students, faculty, and employees. The easiest procedure is to first enroll in a bowling class in the physical education department, learn or review the proper techniques from a qualified instructor, and get acquainted with various types of bowling competition offered by the class. Here you have the advantage of bowling with people of your own age and ability and with whom you become quite well acquainted. This lets you break in to competition in a more relaxed atmosphere.

Next you may wish to consider entering an intramural or student union tournament as a member of a fraternity or dormitory team. These usually are handicap tournaments where, in order to equalize the competition bowlers are given a handicap based on (the more common practice) two-thirds of the difference between the bowler's present averages and 190. For example, a bowler with an average of 145 would have a handicap of 30 (190 minus 145 is 45; two-thirds of 45 is 30). This handicap may change from week to week as new scores are averaged in.

If there is no opportunity for you to bowl on campus, most college communities have commercial lanes in the near vicinity. Many types of leagues or tournaments are in operation both winter and summer. Leagues are established at the request of church groups, commercial businesses, industrial organizations and other occupational groups. These usually are handicap leagues although most bowling centers have at least one "scratch" league for the more advanced men and women bowlers. Organized league bowling is ordinarily sanctioned by the A.B.C. for men, and the W.I.B.C. for women. Persons bowling in such sanctioned leagues must pay a small fee to join the A.B.C. or W.I.B.C. and can establish an official average with the organization.

League teams are made up of four or five bowlers, but two man teams and mixed bowling are also common. Teams usually bowl once a week with each team member rolling three lines per series. To add to the competitive spirit, leagues may collect additional money each week which goes into a prize fund. The prize money is then distributed among the teams and individuals achieving the best scores and records by the end of the season.

Women's or housewives leagues and senior citizens' leagues are popular during the morning and early afternoon hours. Junior leagues for boys and girls are available on Saturday mornings or after school. Since most of the evening hours during the week are reserved for league bowling it is always wise to inquire as to the hours the lanes are available for "open bowling," or phone to see if it is possible to reserve a lane for practice or for an informal game.

If you wish to learn from watching topnotch performers, consult your local bowling establishment or watch for announcements on the sports page of your newspaper for exhibition matches by the professional bowlers or leading tournament teams.

Bowling, like golf, has gained so in popularity with television audiences that not only national tournaments such as the World Invitational from Chicago and the National All-Star events are televised but also on Saturday and Sunday afternoons you can observe exciting matches between the champions.

There are also many films available on a loan or rental basis from the leading bowling equipment companies and other distributors. A list of these plus supplemental reading on bowling can be found in the selected references.

There are several variations of bowling or novelty events that in addition to being fun for parties and a diversion from regular league play are also excellent for sharpening the bowling eye. The following games make use of standard equipment and lanes.

Blind Bowling: A wire with a curtain is hung above the lane about halfway down to block the bowler's view of the pins. Regular scoring is used and the automatic pin machines show the spare set ups remaining. Excellent practice for spot bowling.

Cocked Hat: Set up pins 3-7-10 (right-handers) or 2-7-10 (left-handers). Use two balls per frame as in regular bowling and the scoring is similar except strikes and spares score only three instead of ten points.

Cocked Hat and Feather: Set up pins 1-3-7-10 or 1-2-7-10 and play in the same manner as in the foregoing.

   The 1-5-7-10 can be used with the object being to leave the 5 pin standing. If it should be upset, there is no score in that frame. Both games are good practice for spare bowling but are difficult to arrange with automatic pin machines.

Head Pin: Bowler rolls only one ball per frame, but scores nothing unless the head pin goes down. Score as in regular bowling but of course there are no spares.

Rotation: If no red pin is available, the various numbered pins can be used as the red pin or "IT" pin. Start with #1 on first ball, #2 on second ball, etc. Scored as the foregoing in that the bowler receives nothing unless the particular pin he is shooting for also goes down.

Scotch Doubles: A partnership game, usually mixed doubles where partners roll every other ball throughout the line. Regular scoring is used. A variation in the game allows for a partner to roll the next ball if he or she strikes or spares on the previous ball. The latter game is more enjoyable for men bowlers who have more chances to roll strikes than if they roll in second position and have to do mostly spare bowling.

SELECTED REFERENCES

American Bowling Congress, History of Bowling, Milwaukee, Wisconsin: American Bowling Congress. 1959.

American Machine and Foundry (AMF), Bowling Instructors' Manual. 1962.

Archibald, John J., Bowling for Boys and Girls, Chicago: Follett Publishing Company. 1963.

Bellisimo, Lou, The Bowler's Manual, Englewood Cliffs, New Jersey: Prentice-Hall, Inc.

Canter, Nagy, Ladewig, Fazio and Norris, The Complete Guide to Better Bowling, New York: Maco Magazine Corporation. 1959.

Casady, Donald and Maria Liba, Beginning Bowling, Belmont, California: Wadsworth Publishing Company, 1962.

Day, Ned, How to Bowl, New York: Halcyon House, 1948.

Division for Girls and Women's Sports, Bowling, Fencing and Golf Guide, Washington, D.C.: American Association for Health, Physical Education, and Recreation. 1964-66.

Kidwell, Kathro and Paul Smith, Jr., Bowling Analyzed, Dubuque, Iowa: William C. Brown Company Publishers. 1960.

Miller, Donna Mae and Katherine Ley, Individual and Team Sports for Women, New York: Prentice-Hall, Inc. 1955.

Taylor Dawson, The Secret of Bowling Strikes, New York: A. S. Barnes and Company, Inc. 1960.

Wilman, Joe, Better Bowling, New York: The Ronald Press. 1953.

Women's International Bowling Congress, Inc., League Rule Book, Columbus, Ohio: Women's International Bowling Congress, Inc. 1965-66.

FILMS

BEGINNING BOWLING. 1962. Slidefilm, 35 mm., 60 min., sd., color. Sale: $43.00; rental: $2.50 (2)

BOWLING ACES; SET 'EM UP; STRIKES AND SPARES. 16 mm., 9, 10, and 12 min., b&w. Rental: $3.95 (4)

BOWLING FUNDAMENTALS; STRIKING CHAMPIONS. 16 mm., 15 and 12 min., sd., b&w. Rental $3.95 (4)

LET'S GO BOWLING. 16 mm., 30 min., sd., b&w. Sale: $65.00 (3)

TENPIN SHOWCASE. 1961. 16 mm., 18 min., sd. b&w. Free Loan (1)

FILM DISTRIBUTORS

(1) AMF Pinspotters, Inc., Jericho Turnpike, Westbury, L.I., N.Y.: 6500 N. Lincoln, Chicago, Ill.

(2) Athletic Institute, Merchandise Mart, Room 805, Chicago 54, Ill.

(3) Bowling Proprietors Association of America, 111 S. Washington, Park Ridge, Ill.

(4) ROA's Films, 1696 North Astor St., Milwaukee 2, Wis.

Index

Aim, 23
  combination, 23
  line, 23, 26
  missing point of, 44
  pin bowling, 23
  point of, 26
  spot bowling, 23
Action, 36, 37
Alley, 51
American Bowling Congress, 1, 4, 5, 49, 51, 57, 67
American Junior Bowling Congress, 7, 49
Anchor, 51
Angle, 11, 19, 23, 24, 28, 29, 30, 32, 33, 36, 37
Approach, 4, 11, 12, 21, 51
  cleanliness of, 62
  delivery, 14, 20
  first step, 13, 15, 16, 17
  five step, 13
  four step, 12, 13
  fourth step, 18, 19
  second step, 15, 16, 17
  third step, 17, 18
  three step, 13
Arm Swing Pattern, 15, 43

Back up, 14, 36, 50
Balance, 10, 20, 21, 25, 41, 42
Ball, 63
  color, 64
  drilling, 64
  finger tip, 64
  fit, 63
  house, 63
  thumb hole, 64
  two-fingered, 64
  weight, 63
Bedposts, 52
Big four, 52
Blind, 52
Blind bowling, 68
Blow, 52
Boccie, 46
Bolla, 46
Bolle, 46
Boule, 46
Bowling
  appeal, 4
  averages, 66, 67

centers, 2
charges, 4
equipment, 4, 63
films, 68, 70
history, 46
novelty events, 68
object of, 1
opportunity, 66
popularity, 3
prizes, 67
pro, 4
purposes, 1
Bulla, 46
Bridge, 50
"Brooklyn," 31, 50
Bucket, 52

Check points, 20, 24, 25
Cherry, 29, 30, 52
Choke, 51
Clothing, 6, 7, 65
Cocked hat, 68
Cocked hat & feather, 68
Compensation, 41
Concentration, 11
Conditioning, 40
Creeper, 50
Cross over, 50
Curve, 14, 37

Dead ball, 50, 58, 59
Dead wood, 58, 59
Deflection, 29, 30, 37
Delivery, 14, 27
Double, 52, 56
Double pinochle, 52
Drifting, 41
Dutchman, 52

Error, 52, 54
Equipment, 4, 63
  bag, 64, 65
  balls, 5, 7, 63
  gloves, 65
  personal, 64, 65
  pins, 5, 62
  shoes, 62, 63, 64, 65
Etiquette, 60
  approach, 61
  body English, 60
  equipment, 61

foul line, 61
lanes, 61
priority, 60
sportsmanship, 61

Faults, 42, 43
Feet, 11
Film, 68
distributors, 70
Fingers, 8, 11, 14, 15, 18, 19, 21, 26, 35, 36, 64
"Fit ins," 33
Flat apple, 50
Follow through, 19, 20, 42
Foul, 51, 54, 57, 58
Foul line, 4, 10, 11, 13, 15, 17, 18, 21, 25, 28, 51
Frame, 1, 52, 54, 57
tenth, 56
Full roller, 35
Full spinner, 36

Graveyard, 51
Grip, 7, 11, 13, 15, 21, 35, 40, 64
Gutter ball, 50

Handicap, 52, 67
Headpin, 52, 69
Hints, 44, 45, 56
Holding, 5, 37, 51
Hole, 8, 11
Hook, 13, 14, 15, 19, 23, 25, 26, 28, 34, 50

Irving, W., 48

Kegler, 47, 51
Kickback, 33, 51
King pin, 30, 52

Lane
alley bed, 4
approach, 4
ball return, 5
conditions, 5, 28, 37
construction, 5
dimensions, 4
foul line, 4
gutter, 5
"holding," 5, 37, 51
pit, 5
rack, 5
range finder, 5, 26
"running," 5, 37, 51
"soft," 51
"stiff," 51
Left handed, 8, 10, 64, 65
Lift, 35
Line, 52, 54
Loft, 50, 61
Luther, M., 48

Mark, 52

Novelty events, 68
blind bowling, 68
cocked hat, 68
cocked hat & feather, 68
head pin, 69
rotation, 69
Scotch doubles, 69

Open frame, 53

Pendulum motion, 15, 18
Perfect game, 1, 57
Petrie, Sir F., 46
Physical education, 66
Pin fall, 58
illegal, 58
legal, 58
Pitch, 37, 50, 64
Pocket, 1-3, 21, 23, 24, 26, 29, 30, 31, 36, 37

Rack, 60, 61
Railroad, 39, 52
Range finder, 26, 51
Relaxation, 11
Replacement of pins, 59
Return, 51
Rogers, Dr. M., 46
Rotation, 69
Rules, 57
fouls, 57

Score, 1, 54, 66
Scratch, 53
Scotch doubles, 69
Semi-roller, 34
Semi-spinner, 35
"Shadow bowling," 45
"Sidewheeling," 41
Skills
approach, 12
backswing, 17, 18, 43
basic, 9
"check points," 20
follow through, 19, 20, 21
forward swing, 18, 19
grip, 7, 11, 21
learning of, 6
picking up ball, 9
push away, 11, 15, 17
stance, 10, 21
swing patterns, 15, 16, 17
"Sleeper," 30, 52
Slide, 17, 18, 19
Span, 8, 50
Spares, 27, 28, 53, 54
"covering," 29
definition of, 53
left side, 28, 29, 30, 31
middle, 28, 30
picking up, 27, 28, 29
right side, 28, 29, 32

INDEX

scoring of, 54, 56
Spin, 21, 36, 37
Splits, 27, 33, 38, 51, 54
  baby, 52
  scoring of, 54
Spot, 20, 23, 26, 28, 30, 51
Starting position, 10, 25
Step pattern, 15
Straight ball, 14, 21, 27, 35
Strategy, 38
Strike, 23, 30, 38, 53, 54, 55
Strike out, 53
Substitute, 57
Sweeper, 50

Taps, 34, 52
Target, 10, 11, 19, 20, 23

Team, 1, 38, 39, 57, 60, 67
Television, 4, 44, 68
Terminology, 50
Three quarter roller, 34
Thumb, 8, 11, 14, 15, 19, 21, 26, 35, 36,
  64
Timing, 15, 17, 18, 42, 61
Track, 35, 37
Turkey, 39, 53, 57

Values, 1

Warm ups, 40
Washout, 52
Women's International Bowling Congress,
  1, 49, 51, 57, 67
Woolworth, 52
Working ball, 50